Global SME News Winter 2025–26 Special Edition

MSMEs in a Fragmenting Global Economy

TDW Productions & Publishing

MSMEs in a Fragmenting Global Economy

Global SME News
Winter 2025–26 Special Edition

Edited by Perumal Koshy

Published by TDW Productions & Publishing
Year: 2026
New Delhi, India

ISBN: 978-93-91828-82-0

For permissions, inquiries, or reprint requests, please contact:
info@tdwpublishing.com
Web: https://tdwpublishing.com/

GLOBAL SME NEWS

Global SME News is an independent knowledge and insights publication dedicated to the evolving landscape of micro, small and medium enterprises, entrepreneurship ecosystems, innovation, digital transformation, and enterprise policy developments across regions. The publication brings together perspectives from practitioners, researchers, policy analysts, and industry experts to examine emerging trends shaping enterprise growth, competitiveness, and resilience in a rapidly changing global economy.

Website
www.globalsmenews.com

Published by
TDW Production and Publishing
New Delhi, India
www.tdwpublishing.com

CONTENTS

GLOBAL SME NEWS

https://globalsmenews.com/

Winter 2025–2026

EDITORIAL & GLOBAL PERSPECTIVES

CONTENTS

CONTENTS

STRATEGIC MANAGEMENT & INNOVATION

CONTENTS

CONTENTS

CONTENTS

FUTURE TRENDS & SPECIALIZED REPORTS

CONTENTS

Global SME Perspective

Resilience in a Fragmented Global Economy

The New Operating Reality for Small Enterprise

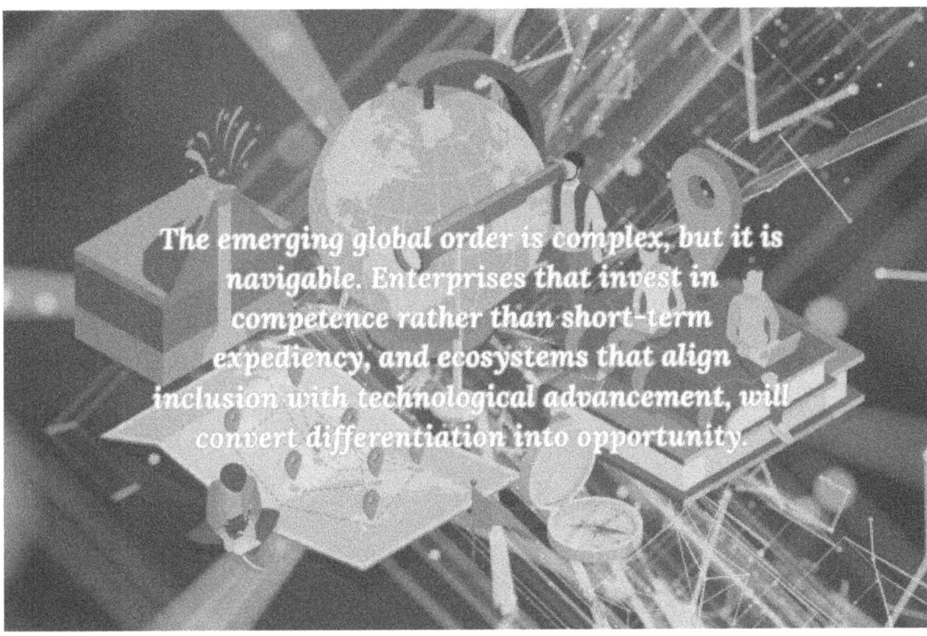

The global economic environment confronting small and medium enterprises is not defined by collapse, nor by simple recovery. It is defined by reconfiguration. Trade architectures are becoming layered rather than uniform. Digital systems are expanding while regulatory regimes tighten. Financial flows are accelerating even as risk screening intensifies. Industrial policy has returned to the centre of national strategy. In this evolving order, small enterprises are not peripheral actors; they are structural participants whose adaptability will shape the durability of growth itself.

For nearly three decades, enterprise internationalisation operated within a broadly liberalising framework. Tariff reduction, logistics optimisation, and digital connectivity reduced entry barriers for smaller firms. Global value chains expanded, and participation became a central development objective. Today, integration persists, but it is mediated through differentiated regulatory blocs, industrial incentive schemes, data governance regimes, and sector-specific standards. Market access is no longer assumed. It is negotiated, documented, and continuously reassessed.

This structural shift alters the calculus of competitiveness. Cost efficiency alone is insufficient. Regulatory literacy, compliance management, cybersecurity discipline, and digital readiness now function as core capabilities. The small enterprise of 2026 must interpret rules of origin, navigate divergent data protection laws, manage cross-border payment protocols, and absorb evolving environmental and reporting standards. The transaction costs of participation have risen, particularly for firms operating with limited managerial bandwidth and constrained access to advisory ecosystems.

Digitalisation, often framed as an equaliser, has become a dual-edged instrument. Cloud platforms, digital payments, artificial intelligence tools, and data-driven analytics offer measurable productivity gains. Automated accounting compresses administrative time. Predictive systems refine inventory management. Digital marketplaces extend geographic reach. For enterprises with stable infrastructure and trained personnel, these tools operate as multipliers of efficiency and resilience.

Yet the diffusion of these technologies is uneven. Digital readiness varies across regions, sectors, and enterprise sizes. Micro-enterprises in informal clusters, rural production networks, and resource-constrained environments often remain in early stages of basic digitisation. Advanced analytics and AI integration risk becoming second-order advantages available primarily to digitally mature firms. The question confronting policymakers and ecosystem leaders is not whether technology will advance, but whether its distribution will reinforce or narrow structural divides within the SME segment itself.

Financial architecture compounds these pressures. The global financing gap for small enterprises remains substantial. In an environment marked by currency volatility, selective trade finance, and heightened risk screening, smaller firms face tighter credit conditions and higher hedging costs. Digital payment systems accelerate settlement cycles and enhance transaction transparency, yet they introduce new exposure to cyber fraud, data governance complexity, and platform dependency. Liquidity has become intertwined with technological infrastructure.

Cyber risk, once perceived as a concern for large corporations, now directly threatens small enterprise continuity. Supply chains are interconnected. SMEs frequently serve as access points within broader networks. A breach in a small firm can cascade through an ecosystem. Digital protection is therefore not a discretionary expenditure but embedded infrastructure. Risk management has shifted from perimeter defence toward continuous verification models, layered safeguards, and behavioural awareness. Enterprises that treat cybersecurity as a strategic function rather than a technical afterthought will possess a decisive advantage in maintaining trust within regulated value chains.

Simultaneously, industrial policy has re-emerged as a central organising principle in many economies. Clean energy transitions, advanced manufacturing incentives, digital public infrastructure, and strategic technology investments are reshaping production geographies. These shifts create both thresholds and openings. Higher environmental, social, and governance standards raise entry barriers. Certification costs and reporting obligations can deter smaller suppliers. Yet diversification strategies and regional production realignment generate selective opportunities for agile firms capable of meeting upgraded requirements. Industrial transformation is also altering labour demand. Automation reorganises tasks but does not eliminate sectors anchored in demographic momentum and structural necessity. Healthcare, education, renewable energy deployment, infrastructure retrofitting, agri-processing, environmental services, and community-based enterprises continue to expand. Artificial intelligence modifies workflows; it does not remove the need for contextual judgment, ethical discretion, and human interaction. Employment reallocation within sectors is underway, but the small enterprise remains central to service delivery, localisation, and innovation diffusion.

In this differentiated landscape, resilience cannot be reduced to survival tactics. It requires embedded strategic alignment. Enterprises must evaluate exposure across multiple dimensions: regulatory, technological, financial, and operational. Diversifying supplier networks, investing in compliance capability, integrating secure digital systems, and cultivating data literacy are no longer aspirational enhancements. They are foundational conditions for sustained participation.

Public policy must evolve in parallel. Traditional SME promotion tools—credit guarantees, cluster development, generic training programmes—are insufficient if disconnected from transnational compliance realities. Integrated ecosystems are required: trade facilitation linked with digital governance training; affordable cybersecurity capacity-building; tiered regulatory frameworks proportionate to enterprise scale; accessible advisory platforms explaining complex trade agreements and standards. Fragmented institutional guidance in a fragmented global economy compounds vulnerability.

The global system has not retreated from interconnectedness. It has reorganised into layered and differentiated channels. For small enterprises, the central challenge is navigating multiplicity without scale advantages. Adaptive competitiveness—defined by regulatory awareness, digital integration, financial prudence, and strategic positioning within regional corridors—will determine which firms consolidate gains and which struggle against rising thresholds.

Resilience, in this context, is neither defensive nor static. It is dynamic capability. It involves interpreting change early, reallocating resources efficiently, and embedding risk management into everyday decision-making. It requires leadership that recognises digital protection as governance, technology as infrastructure, and compliance as market access rather than administrative burden.

Small enterprises constitute the majority of businesses worldwide and a substantial share of employment. Their capacity to operate confidently within differentiated systems will shape broader economic stability. The current phase of transformation is structural, not cyclical. It demands clarity of strategy and coherence of institutional support.

The emerging global order is complex, but it is navigable. Enterprises that invest in competence rather than short-term expediency, and ecosystems that align inclusion with technological advancement, will convert differentiation into opportunity. The measure of the coming decade will not be the pace of disruption alone, but the quality of adaptation across the small enterprise landscape.

African Union Strengthens Delivery Framework Under Agenda 2063

The African Union has intensified implementation of Agenda 2063 under its Second Ten-Year Implementation Plan (2024–2033), marking what policymakers describe as a "Decade of Acceleration" toward structural transformation, continental integration, and inclusive growth.

At the recent AU Summit, Member States adopted "Assuring Sustainable Water Availability and Safe Sanitation Systems" as the 2026 Theme of the Year, positioning water security and sanitation infrastructure as foundational drivers of economic productivity, food systems resilience, public health, and climate adaptation. The focus aligns with broader industrialisation and human capital objectives embedded in Agenda 2063.

Continental integration also moved higher on the political agenda, with renewed calls for faster ratification and operationalisation of the Protocol on Free Movement of Persons to unlock gains under the African Continental Free Trade Area. Improved mobility is viewed as essential for regional value chains, services trade, and SME cross-border participation.

In parallel, the AU Commission convened a High-Level Africa Private Sector Forum, reinforcing the role of enterprise ecosystems in financing and delivering Agenda 2063 priorities. Discussions emphasised infrastructure investment, digital transformation, and innovative financing mechanisms as critical enablers of implementation.

As Agenda 2063 advances into its acceleration phase, policy attention is increasingly shifting from vision-setting to measurable delivery — with integration, infrastructure, and private sector mobilisation at the centre of continental strategy.

Source: https://au.int/en/agenda2063/overview

AU Leaders Renew Commitment to Industrialisation and Intra-African Trade

At the 39th Ordinary Session of the Assembly of the African Union in February 2026, heads of state consolidated a central economic priority: industrialisation anchored in regional value chains with structured participation of small and medium enterprises. The deliberations moved beyond declaratory support for integration and focused on strengthening productive systems capable of sustaining intra-African trade and export diversification.

Recommitment to Agenda 2063 implementation was positioned within a production-led growth framework. Leaders underscored that trade integration must be accompanied by domestic capacity building—industrial upgrading, technology diffusion, logistics connectivity, and standards harmonisation—if continental trade frameworks are to generate tangible economic transformation.

Operational acceleration of the African Continental Free Trade Area was reaffirmed, particularly in relation to enabling SMEs to embed within cross-border supply chains. Emphasis was placed on value addition, sectoral clustering, and alignment of national industrial policies with continental trade instruments.

The summit's central message was clear: sustainable integration requires shifting from commodity dependence toward coordinated manufacturing and services ecosystems in which SMEs function as active nodes within regional production networks rather than peripheral actors.

http://www.ihsfairplay.com/Maritime_Data/maritime_data.html

The BRICS grouping has formally adopted the SME Working Group Action

Plan 2025–2030, marking the first structured multilateral roadmap dedicated specifically to micro, small and medium enterprise cooperation within the bloc. The framework was endorsed under the BRICS Industry Ministers' process and aligned with summit-level commitments to deepen industrial collaboration and economic coordination.

The Action Plan establishes a designated SME Working Group with defined terms of reference and multi-year priorities. It provides a platform for systematic policy dialogue, institutional exchange, and coordination among member states on enterprise development frameworks. Areas of focus include strengthening productive capacity, expanding SME participation in cross-border trade, promoting digital integration, enhancing skills development, and supporting technology adoption.

By embedding SME cooperation within the broader industrial and economic agenda of BRICS, the initiative signals a policy shift toward structured enterprise-level engagement rather than general trade declarations alone. The framework recognises SMEs as critical drivers of employment generation, value-chain diversification, and innovation across member economies.

For smaller firms operating in complex regulatory and financial environments, coordinated approaches on digital standards, financing mechanisms, and market access procedures can reduce transaction uncertainty and enhance predictability in cross-bloc engagement. The Action Plan does not replace national SME programmes but creates an intergovernmental platform through which policy practices, data, and implementation models can be shared.

Given the economic weight of BRICS economies in global trade and manufacturing output, formalising SME cooperation through a five-year roadmap represents a measurable institutional development. Its practical impact will depend on how member states translate working group coordination into operational measures—particularly in areas such as trade facilitation, digital interoperability, financing instruments, and export support structures.

Sources

- *BRICS SME Working Group Action Plan 2025–2030 (Official Document)https://brics.br/pt-br/documentos/economia-financas-comercio-e-infraestrutura/sme-action-plan-2025-2030-wg.pdf*
- *Rio de Janeiro Declaration – BRICS Summit 2025https://www.pmindia.gov.in/en/news_updates/rio-de-janeiro-declaration-strengthening-global-south-cooperation-for-a-more-inclusive-and-sustainable-governance/*
- *BRICS Industry Ministers' Meeting Documentation (Brazil Chairship 2025)https://www.gov.br/memp/pt-br/assuntos/brics-sme-working-group-1*
- *BRICS Policy Report on Digital Transformation and Industrial Cooperation https://cetic.br/media/docs/publicacoes/1/20250522114346/digital_trans*formation_in_age_of_ai.pdf

Eurasian Economic Union: Policy and Trade Developments (2025–2026)

The Eurasian Economic Union (EAEU) approved its Main Guidelines for Macroeconomic Policy for 2026–2027 at the meeting of the Supreme Eurasian Economic Council in December 2025. The document outlines coordinated macroeconomic priorities among member states, including economic stability, balanced growth, and further integration within the internal market framework.

In parallel, the Heads of State endorsed the Main Directions of International Activities of the EAEU for 2026, setting priorities for expanded trade and economic cooperation with partner countries and regional groupings in Asia, the Middle East, Africa and Latin America. Continued institutional engagement with multilateral bodies, including the World Trade Organization, remains part of the external agenda. On 20 August 2025, India and the EAEU signed the Terms of Reference to launch negotiations on a Free Trade Agreement (FTA). The negotiations, structured under an agreed roadmap, are focused primarily on goods trade. India's trade turnover with the EAEU was reported at approximately USD 69 billion in 2024.

The EAEU also continued implementation of the 2018 Agreement on Trade and Economic Cooperation with China. Meetings of the joint commission in 2025–2026 addressed regulatory coordination, trade facilitation measures and standards-related issues under the existing cooperation framework.In addition, the Eurasian Economic Commission (EEC) reported expansion of statistical monitoring mechanisms from 2026 onward, including compilation of economic and integration indicators submitted by member states to support policy coordination.

Sources

- *Eurasian Economic Commission. "Main Guidelines for Macroeconomic Policy of the EAEU Member States for 2026–2027." December 2025.https://eec.eaeunion.org/en/news/utverzhdeny-osnovnye-orientiry-makroekonomicheskoy-politiki-gosudarstv-eaes-na-2026-2027-gody/*
- *Eurasian Economic Commission. "Main Directions of International Activities of the EAEU for 2026." December 2025.https://eec.eaeunion.org/en/news/utverzhdeny-osnovnye-napravleniya-mezhdunarodnoy-deyatelnosti-eaes-na-2026-god/*
- *Eurasian Economic Commission. Statement following EAEU–China Joint Commission Meeting. 2025.https://eec.eaeunion.org/news/andrey-slepnev-na-sovmestnoy-komissii-eaes-knr-predlozheny-resheniya-po-klyuchevym-voprosam-povestki/*

EU InvestEU Boosts Space-Tech Venture Debt, Expands SME Finance Pathways

The European Commission and European Investment Bank (EIB) have deployed a €25 million InvestEU venture-debt package to support OQ Technology's next-generation satellite communications platform. This financing will accelerate development of low-Earth-orbit connectivity capable of delivering 5G and IoT services directly to devices — a strategic step in Europe's space-tech ecosystem.

For small and medium enterprises, the use of venture debt backed by public guarantees illustrates an emerging financing model that can bridge persistent capital gaps — particularly for high-growth, innovation-led firms that struggle with conventional credit criteria. By reducing reliance on collateral and embracing risk-sharing, such instruments broaden SME access to finance and support competitiveness in strategic technology domains.

This arrangement signals a broader shift in enterprise finance: public-mission programmes are increasingly integrating structured capital solutions tailored to innovation cycles rather than asset-based lending alone. For SMEs operating at the intersection of digital services and infrastructure, these developments point to scalable, non-dilutive pathways to fund growth, expand market reach, and participate in technologically differentiated value chains.

Source: https://ec.europa.eu/

EU Advances Digital Omnibus to Ease SME Compliance Across Data and AI Rules

The European Commission has proposed a Digital Omnibus package designed to streamline overlapping digital regulations across data protection, artificial intelligence, and related digital frameworks within the European Union. The initiative aims to reduce administrative burdens, improve regulatory coherence, and enhance business competitiveness across the Digital Single Market.

For SMEs operating across borders, fragmented compliance requirements have often translated into disproportionate legal and administrative costs. By simplifying reporting structures and aligning digital obligations, the proposal seeks to lower transaction friction and make regulatory navigation more predictable — particularly for smaller firms without dedicated compliance teams.

If adopted, the Digital Omnibus could represent a structural shift toward regulatory rationalisation, reinforcing the EU's attempt to balance innovation, digital governance, and enterprise competitiveness within an increasingly complex technological landscape.

Source: https://ec.europa.eu

EU Allocates €1.4 Billion Under 2026 Innovation Council Programme to Strengthen Deep-Tech SMEs

The European Commission has adopted the 2026 Work Programme of the European Innovation Council (EIC), committing €1.4 billion to support breakthrough technologies and high-growth innovative enterprises across the European Union. The programme combines grants and equity-style investment instruments to accelerate the transition from research to commercial scale.

For SMEs operating in deep-tech sectors, the EIC framework addresses a persistent structural constraint: limited access to scale-up capital during high-risk innovation phases. By blending public funding with market-oriented investment mechanisms, the initiative strengthens pathways for technology commercialisation, cross-border expansion, and investor readiness. The 2026 allocation reinforces the EU's strategic emphasis on innovation-led competitiveness, positioning smaller technology enterprises as central actors in Europe's industrial and digital transformation agenda.

Source: https://ec.europa.eu

United Arab Emirates: National Agenda for Entrepreneurship and SMEs

The United Arab Emirates has launched a National Agenda for Entrepreneurship and SMEs as a central pillar of its economic diversification and competitiveness strategy, with the objective of positioning the UAE among the world's leading entrepreneurial ecosystems by 2031.

The Agenda consists of 29 integrated initiatives structured around regulatory reform, financing access, innovation capacity, market expansion and institutional coordination. A core component focuses on improving the ease of doing business through streamlined licensing procedures, simplified regulatory requirements, enhanced insolvency and restructuring frameworks, and digitalisation of business registration and compliance systems.

Access to finance is addressed through expansion of credit guarantee schemes, support for venture capital and growth equity markets, promotion of fintech-enabled lending platforms, and development of alternative financing instruments for startups and scale-ups. The framework also emphasises improving SME participation in federal and local government procurement, including supplier development and localisation initiatives.

Innovation and ecosystem development measures include strengthening incubator and accelerator networks, sector-focused entrepreneurship clusters, university–industry collaboration, and targeted support for technology-based enterprises. Export readiness and internationalisation support are also included to facilitate SME entry into global markets, particularly within priority trade corridors.

Institutionally, the Agenda promotes coordination between federal and emirate-level entities to ensure policy coherence and reduce duplication across regulatory jurisdictions. It is aligned with broader national strategies aimed at increasing the contribution of SMEs to GDP, expanding non-oil economic activity, and reinforcing the UAE's position as a regional hub for innovation, digital enterprise and knowledge-based industries.

Source: *UAE Ministry of Economy & Tourism. National Agenda for Entrepreneurship and SMEs (2025).https://www.moet.gov.ae/en/uae-business-ecosystem*

United States: SBA Finalizes SBIC Program Reforms

The U.S. Small Business Administration (SBA) finalized regulatory reforms to the Small Business Investment Company (SBIC) program on 14 January 2026. The updated rule revises eligibility criteria, removes certain legacy regulatory provisions, and streamlines participation requirements for private investment funds operating under the SBIC framework.

The reforms are intended to facilitate increased private capital flows into small businesses, including enterprises operating in advanced manufacturing, critical technologies and other strategic sectors. The SBIC program, which leverages federal guarantees to mobilise private investment into small firms, remains one of the primary federal mechanisms supporting long-term equity financing for growth-oriented SMEs.

According to the SBA, the regulatory updates aim to improve program efficiency, clarify compliance standards, and enhance capital deployment capacity within the SBIC structure.

Source

- *U.S. Small Business Administration. "SBA Finalizes SBIC Reforms to Fuel Private Investment in Critical Industries." 14 January 2026. https://www.sba.gov/article/2026/01/14/sba-finalizes-sbic-reforms-fuel-private-investment-critical-industries*

Asia: Startup Ecosystems and Funding Availability and Institutions

Asian startup ecosystems are transitioning from high-liquidity expansion to structured consolidation. Across ASEAN and South Asia, governments are reinforcing co-investment models, sovereign participation, regulatory sandboxes, and digital public infrastructure to sustain capital flows while strengthening governance and long-term viability.

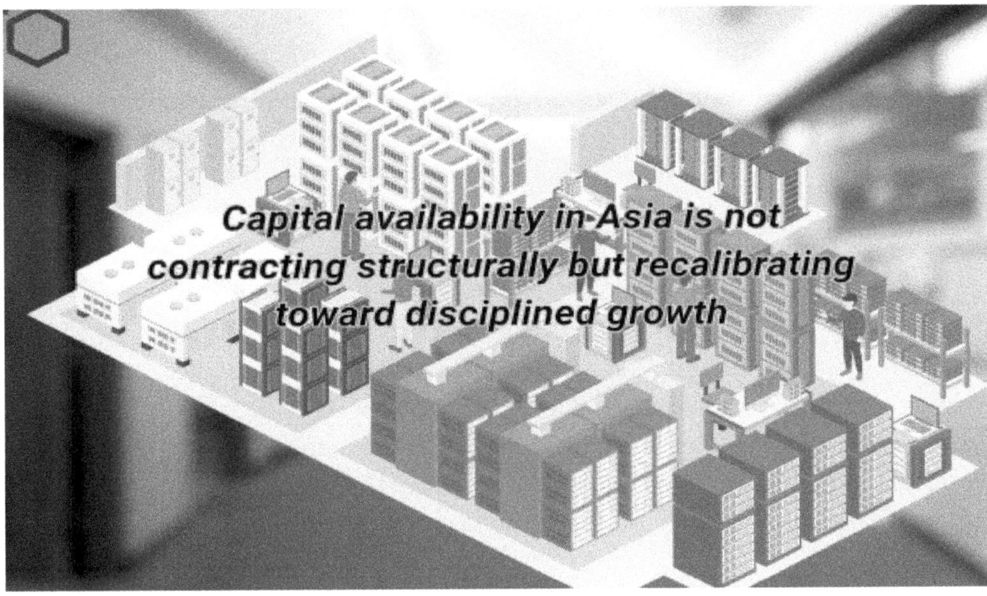

In Singapore, the financing architecture remains one of the most institutionally mature in Asia. Through Enterprise Singapore and the Startup SG Equity scheme, the state co-invests alongside private venture capital, reducing early-stage risk and crowding in private participation. Budget 2026 further strengthened SME internationalisation grants and AI capability development support, reinforcing outward-oriented growth and technology upgrading.

In India, the Startup India framework continues to anchor the ecosystem, now exceeding 200,000 DPIIT-recognised startups. The Fund of Funds for Startups, managed by Small Industries Development Bank of India, catalyses domestic venture capital while leveraging public capital to expand equity access. Digital Public Infrastructure—particularly UPI and related digital platforms—continues lowering transaction and onboarding costs. Funding has become more valuation-disciplined since 2023, with policy attention shifting toward deep-tech, manufacturing-linked innovation, and tier-II ecosystem expansion.

In Indonesia, startup growth remains closely tied to fintech and digital commerce. Regulatory sandboxes under Otoritas Jasa Keuangan support innovation while tightening prudential standards. MSME digital onboarding programmes are expanding formal financing pathways, especially for platform-based enterprises.

In Vietnam, innovation policy is integrated with industrial upgrading strategies. The National Innovation Center promotes startup incubation, technology transfer, and value-chain integration aligned with FDI inflows. SME digital transformation and productivity upgrading remain policy priorities.

Across ASEAN and South Asia, five structural trends are visible: expansion of sovereign-backed co-investment funds; greater regulatory oversight through sandbox frameworks; integration of digital public infrastructure; emphasis on export readiness and regional value chains; and stronger scrutiny of profitability and governance standards. Venture capital flows remain below peak 2021–22 levels, but early-stage pipelines in AI, climate technology, fintech, and industrial innovation continue to attract institutional backing.

Overall, capital availability in Asia is not contracting structurally but recalibrating toward disciplined growth. Institutional participation—rather than purely private venture cycles—is now the defining characteristic of the region's startup financing environment.

Sources

- *Enterprise Singapore – Startup SG Equity: https://www.enterprisesg.gov.sg*
- *Singapore Ministry of Finance – Budget 2026: https://www.mof.gov.sg*
- *Startup India (Government of India): https://www.startupindia.gov.in*
- *Small Industries Development Bank of India – Fund of Funds for Startups: https://www.sidbi.in*
- *Otoritas Jasa Keuangan (Indonesia) – Regulatory Sandbox Framework: https://www.ojk.go.id*
- *Ministry of Cooperatives and SMEs (Indonesia): https://www.kemenkopukm.go.id*
- *National Innovation Center (Vietnam): https://nic.gov.vn*
- *Ministry of Planning and Investment (Vietnam): https://www.mpi.gov.vn*
- *CB Insights – Venture Trends Southeast Asia: https://www.cbinsights.com/research/report/venture-capital-southeast-asia-trends/*
- *DealStreetAsia – Funding and Startup Reports: https://www.dealstreetasia.com/stories/*

Cybersecurity insurance offers vital financial protection for SMEs, covering losses from business interruptions, regulatory fines, legal costs, and reputational damage. In today's threat-heavy digital landscape, it's not a backup plan — it's a critical pillar of enterprise risk management.

Cyber Insurance: A Critical Shield for SMEs

In today's hyperconnected economy, cyber risk is no longer confined to large corporations with complex digital infrastructures. Small and medium enterprises have become deeply embedded in digital ecosystems through cloud services, online platforms, mobile payments, digital supply chains, and remote work arrangements. As a result, cybersecurity incidents now pose a direct and often existential threat to SME continuity, resilience, and long-term viability. SMEs are increasingly attractive targets for cybercriminals precisely because of their structural vulnerabilities. Compared to large firms, they typically operate with limited cybersecurity budgets, minimal in-house technical expertise, and fragmented digital governance frameworks. Recent global assessments indicate that approximately 43 percent of reported cyber incidents worldwide involve

SMEs, while nearly one-third of ransomware attacks explicitly target smaller businesses.

The situation is even more acute in emerging digital economies, where close to 70 percent of SMEs report having no formal preparedness or response mechanisms in place to deal with cyberattacks. These gaps expose enterprises to cascading risks that extend well beyond temporary disruption. For many SMEs, a single cyber incident can trigger a chain of consequences—loss of sensitive data, prolonged operational downtime, regulatory penalties, erosion of customer trust, and severe liquidity stress.

In extreme cases, cyber incidents have resulted in permanent business closure, particularly where enterprises lack financial buffers or access to emergency capital. Unlike large corporations, SMEs often do not have the balance sheet resilience or legal capacity to absorb such shocks. Against this backdrop, cyber insurance is emerging as a critical pillar of SME risk management rather than a discretionary add-on. At its core, cyber insurance functions as a financial risk transfer mechanism, absorbing a range of costs that SMEs would otherwise be unable to bear.

These include expenses associated with data breaches, regulatory compliance and penalties, loss of revenue due to business interruption, ransomware and cyber extortion demands, legal defense and forensic investigations, as well as crisis communication and reputation management. Modern cyber insurance policies designed for SMEs typically extend beyond narrow indemnification.

They increasingly integrate response-oriented services that help enterprises manage the immediate aftermath of an incident. This includes support for breach containment, notification of affected customers or partners, forensic analysis to identify the source and scope of the attack, and access to legal expertise to navigate regulatory obligations. In cases of ransomware, coverage may include not only ransom payments but also negotiation support and recovery assistance, which can significantly reduce downtime. Several global insurers have developed cyber insurance offerings tailored specifically to the operational realities of SMEs.

These solutions emphasize modular coverage structures, flexible policy limits, and bundled access to incident response specialists. While global insurers differ in geographic focus and service depth, a common trend is the recognition that SMEs require simplified, scalable policies that align with their digital exposure rather than enterprise-grade complexity. For SME executives, founders, and CIOs, selecting appropriate cyber insurance requires strategic judgment rather than a purely compliance-driven approach. Coverage must be aligned with the enterprise's actual digital footprint, including its dependence on cloud services, customer data volumes, and regulatory environment. Particular attention should be paid to ransomware protection and business interruption coverage, as these represent the most financially damaging categories of cyber incidents for small firms.

Equally important is ensuring rapid access to incident response expertise, as speed of response often determines whether a cyber event becomes a manageable disruption or a catastrophic failure. Cost considerations remain critical for SMEs, but affordability should be assessed in relation to risk exposure rather than short-term savings. Cyber insurance is most effective when integrated into a broader cybersecurity strategy that includes basic digital hygiene, employee awareness, and minimum security controls.

Insurance does not replace cybersecurity investments; rather, it complements them by providing financial and operational backstopping when defenses fail. As SMEs continue to digitize operations and integrate into global digital markets, cyber risk will increasingly shape competitive outcomes. In this context, embedding cyber insurance within enterprise risk management frameworks is not merely prudent but essential. Looking ahead to 2025 and beyond, SMEs that proactively integrate cyber risk mitigation—including insurance—into their strategic planning will be better positioned to withstand digital shocks, maintain stakeholder confidence, and sustain growth in an increasingly volatile cyber landscape.

Starting Drone Business *Aquiline Drones Franchise Program for Veterans**

Hartford, CT – In a move set to transform the drone sector, a new initiative is providing U.S. military veterans with a direct path to entrepreneurship in the rapidly growing unmanned aerial vehicle (UAV) market. Aquiline Drones (AD), a Connecticut-based drone manufacturer and AI systems company, has partnered with Ryder System, Inc. and Vets to Drones to create a discounted drone franchise program specifically for veterans.

This strategic partnership honors the valuable contributions of all U.S. military veterans. By combining forces, they are making these drone franchises more accessible than ever, offering an impressive 30% discount to qualified veterans.

*First published in the web edition of Global SME News**

This significant saving is made possible by Ryder's substantial discounts on franchise vehicles and Vets to Drones' commitment to providing free professional drone training.

A New Chapter for Veterans and the Drone Industry

Aquiline Drones founder and CEO Barry Alexander emphasizes the unparalleled skills that veterans bring to the table. "Veterans bring unmatched discipline, technical expertise, and leadership to the drone industry," says Alexander. This program leverages those skills, creating new opportunities for veterans while strengthening the domestic drone industry.

The initiative aligns with crucial federal programs like the U.S. Department of War's (DoW) Blue UAS program and the Defense Innovation Unit's (DIU) Replicator Initiative. These federal directives aim to boost domestic drone production, reduce reliance on foreign-made platforms, and cultivate a skilled workforce to support defense and commercial missions. Aquiline Drones' veteran-owned franchise model is a key part of this strategy, reinforcing U.S. manufacturing capabilities and building a prepared workforce.

Diverse Franchise Models for a Growing Market

The AD–Vets to Drones initiative offers structured franchise opportunities across three distinct models, each designed to meet a critical market need:

Modular Drone Manufacturing (MDM): This model allows veterans to produce U.S.-made, Blue UAS-compliant drones, positioning them for federal procurement and industrial base contracts.

Inspection, Security & Surveillance (ISS): Franchisees can support missions for agencies like the Department of Homeland Security (DHS), Customs and Border Protection (CBP), and FEMA by providing services such as border surveillance, disaster response, and infrastructure security.

Total Exterior Care (TEC): This model focuses on providing advanced drone services for exterior cleaning, including power-washing, painting, and graffiti removal, as well as environmental monitoring for municipal, industrial, and defense settings.

Each franchise comes with comprehensive support, including professional pilot training, business development assistance, and access to Aquiline Drones Indemnity Corporation (ADIC), a captive insurance entity that provides tailored coverage. Furthermore, franchisees can qualify for federal contracting opportunities as a Veteran-Owned Small Business (VOSB) or a Service-Disabled Veteran-Owned Small Business (SDVOSB).

Veteran Entrepreneurship and National Security

This program is more than just a career path; it's an opportunity for veterans to become business owners and leaders in a vital sector. As Chris Lewis, Founder and CEO of Vets to Drones, notes, "This partnership offers Veterans more than just a career path; it presents the opportunity for ownership in a rapidly growing sector crucial to U.S. defense and economic competitiveness."

The U.S. drone market is projected to exceed $60 billion in the next decade, driven by defense, infrastructure, and commercial applications. The AD–Vets to Drones initiative aims to:

Cultivate Veteran Entrepreneurship: Empowering veterans to transition into ownership roles that boost local economies and advance U.S. technological leadership.

Bolster Homeland Security: Building a national workforce of veteran franchisees to support DHS and DoW missions.

Strengthen the Domestic UAS Industrial Base: Aligning with the DoW's Replicator initiative to scale U.S. production capacity for autonomous UAV systems.

Global Drone Market: Expanding Commercial Ecosystem

The global drone industry continues to transition from predominantly defence-oriented deployment to structured commercial applications across agriculture, infrastructure, energy, logistics and environmental monitoring. Market assessments indicate sustained expansion through 2030, driven by integration of artificial intelligence, advanced sensors, cloud-based data analytics and regulatory adaptation in multiple jurisdictions.

According to Grand View Research, the global drone market was valued at approximately USD 73.06 billion in 2024 and is projected to reach USD 163.60 billion by 2030, reflecting continued enterprise adoption across commercial and industrial segments. Parallel estimates suggest strong growth in the commercial drone services segment, with increasing uptake in precision agriculture, inspection services, mapping and logistics.

Opportunities for small and medium enterprises are emerging across multiple layers of the value chain:

• Drone manufacturing and component assembly (airframes, propulsion systems, payload integration)
• Drone-as-a-Service (DaaS) operations for agriculture, infrastructure inspection and surveying
• AI-driven analytics platforms for aerial data processing
• Maintenance, repair and pilot training services
• Compliance advisory and certification services in regulated airspace environments

Skill requirements span aeronautical engineering, embedded systems, GIS mapping, data analytics, AI integration, cybersecurity for unmanned systems, and certified UAV piloting. The services-based model in particular lowers capital barriers compared to full-scale manufacturing, creating entry points for technology-oriented startups and specialised service providers.

As regulatory frameworks mature and industrial digitalisation accelerates, the drone ecosystem is increasingly aligned with smart agriculture, renewable energy monitoring, urban planning and industrial automation — sectors where SME participation remains significant.

Sources

- *Grand View Research. Drone Market Size, Share & Trends Analysis Report (2024–2030)https://www.grandviewresearch.com/industry-analysis/drone-market-report*
- *Grand View Research. Commercial Drone Market Size Report (2025–2030)https://www.grandviewresearch.com/industry-analysis/global-commercial-drones-market*
- *MarketsandMarkets. Unmanned Aerial Vehicle (UAV) Market – Global Forecast to 2030https://www.marketsandmarkets.com/Market-Reports/unmanned-aerial-vehicles-uav-market-662.html*
- *MarkNtel Advisors. Global Drone Services Market Forecasthttps://www.marknteladvisors.com/research-library/global-drone-services-market.html*

Automotive Brake Fluid Market: From Consumable Input to Safety-Critical Technology Segment

Svetlana M

The global automotive brake fluid market is entering a phase of steady but structurally significant growth, reflecting broader transformations within the automotive industry. According to data from Growth Market Reports, the market was valued at approximately USD 3.1 billion in 2024 and is projected to reach USD 4.76 billion by 2033, expanding at a compound annual growth rate (CAGR) of 5.1 percent between 2025 and 2033. While the expansion appears moderate in numerical terms, the underlying drivers indicate a deeper transition—from a commodity-oriented product category toward a technology-sensitive component closely tied to vehicle safety, system integration, and regulatory compliance.

Repositioning Brake Fluid in the Automotive Value Chain

In public discourse around mobility transformation, attention tends to concentrate on electrification, autonomous driving systems, or battery technologies. Yet braking systems remain among the most critical safety subsystems in any vehicle architecture. Brake fluid functions as the hydraulic medium that translates driver input or electronic commands into mechanical stopping force. Its reliability directly affects vehicle control, response time, and operational safety.

Unlike conventional automotive consumables, brake fluid operates under demanding conditions. It must maintain consistent viscosity across temperature extremes, resist moisture absorption, avoid vapor formation at high temperatures, and remain chemically stable over extended service intervals. As braking systems increasingly interact with anti-lock braking systems (ABS), electronic stability control (ESC), advanced driver assistance systems (ADAS), and regenerative braking mechanisms, the functional expectations placed upon brake fluids have expanded considerably.

Technical Evolution and Product Segmentation

The market continues to be dominated by glycol-based fluids, particularly DOT 3, DOT 4, and DOT 5.1 classifications, which offer a balance between performance and cost efficiency. These formulations are widely used in passenger vehicles and light commercial vehicles due to their compatibility with contemporary braking architectures and established manufacturing ecosystems.

Silicone-based fluids, categorized as DOT 5, represent a smaller but stable niche. Their resistance to moisture absorption and longer storage life makes them suitable for specialty applications such as military vehicles or classic automotive segments. However, compatibility limitations with modern braking components restrict their broader adoption.

More recently, hybrid and advanced formulations have begun gaining traction. These products are designed to support low-viscosity performance required by electronically controlled braking systems while maintaining high thermal stability. The shift reflects a growing convergence between chemical engineering and electronic system requirements within vehicle design.

Structural Drivers of Market Growth

Several structural forces are shaping demand patterns within the automotive brake fluid market.

Electrification of vehicle platforms is one of the most significant factors. Electric vehicles rely extensively on regenerative braking, which reduces routine friction braking but introduces higher thermal stress during sudden or high-load braking events. This operational pattern increases the need for fluids capable of maintaining stability despite irregular usage cycles and higher temperature spikes.

Regulatory pressures are also contributing to market evolution. Across major automotive markets, braking performance standards and safety regulations are becoming more stringent, compelling original equipment manufacturers (OEMs) to adopt higher-grade fluids with improved performance characteristics.

At the same time, expansion in global vehicle ownership, particularly across emerging economies, is strengthening aftermarket demand. Brake fluid replacement remains a recurring maintenance requirement, and rising awareness of preventive maintenance is gradually expanding consumption volumes beyond OEM channels.

Innovation at the Intersection of Chemistry and Electronics

Technological innovation within the brake fluid segment is increasingly oriented toward system responsiveness and durability rather than basic hydraulic functionality. Low-viscosity formulations enable faster pressure transmission, which is essential for vehicles equipped with automatic emergency braking and other software-controlled safety features. In such systems, milliseconds of response time can significantly influence stopping distance and accident avoidance outcomes.

Manufacturers are also investing in extended service-life formulations that retain performance characteristics over longer operational cycles. This development aligns with fleet management priorities, where reduced downtime and maintenance intervals translate into operational cost savings.

Sustainability Considerations and Environmental Pressures

Environmental considerations are gradually influencing formulation strategies. Brake fluids contain chemical additives that require careful disposal, and regulatory scrutiny around automotive fluids is increasing in several jurisdictions. Industry efforts are therefore focusing on reducing toxic components, improving degradation characteristics, and extending fluid lifespan to reduce overall consumption volumes.

Although recycling brake fluid remains technically complex due to contamination and chemical stability issues, longer service intervals represent an indirect but practical pathway toward reducing environmental impact.

Regional Market Dynamics

Market dynamics vary significantly across regions. In North America and Europe, growth is largely value-driven, with demand concentrated around premium and OEM-approved formulations supporting advanced braking technologies. Vehicle parc expansion in these regions is relatively stable, limiting volume growth but encouraging product innovation.

In contrast, Asia-Pacific and other emerging automotive markets continue to experience growth driven by rising vehicle ownership, improving service networks, and increasing consumer awareness of vehicle safety standards. These regions are expected to remain central to volume expansion in the coming decade.

Competitive Landscape

The market remains moderately consolidated, with major chemical and energy companies playing dominant roles. Key participants include BASF SE, Robert Bosch GmbH, Dow Inc., Chevron Corporation, FUCHS Petrolub SE, Valvoline Inc., TotalEnergies SE, Shell plc, Castrol Limited, ExxonMobil Corporation, Sinopec, Motul S.A., BP plc, PETRONAS, Lukoil, Repsol S.A., Huntsman Corporation, Sasol Limited, and Blue Star Lubrication Technology Co., Ltd. Competition increasingly revolves around formulation performance, OEM partnerships, and compliance with evolving safety and environmental standards.

Outlook: A Quiet but Strategic Transformation

The automotive brake fluid market is gradually transitioning from a maintenance-oriented consumables segment into a technologically differentiated safety domain. Future demand will be shaped by software-controlled braking systems, autonomous vehicle safety requirements, and the thermal challenges associated with heavier electrified vehicle architectures. At the same time, growing consumer awareness around preventive maintenance is likely to reinforce aftermarket demand.

Brake fluid may remain largely invisible to end users, but its technological evolution reflects a broader truth about modern mobility: as vehicles become more intelligent and complex, even the most understated components assume strategic importance in ensuring safety and reliability.

First published in the web edition of Global SME News <https://globalsmenews.com/automotive-brake-fluid-market-from-consumable-input-to-safety-critical-technology-segment/

Trust, Tenure and Growth

Rungta Tea's Expansion Story

Rungta Tea marks 24 years in India's FMCG sector with an exceptional 92% distributor retention rate, underscoring a relationship-led distribution model built on quality, transparency, and trust. With strong manufacturing capabilities in Siliguri and rising demand for its Real Gold brand across North and East India, the company is now gearing up for accelerated expansion backed by infrastructure designed for long-term scale.

In an industry characterized by frequent churn and intense competitive pressures, Rungta Tea has reported a 92 percent distributor retention rate sustained over 24 years of operations, a performance that stands out in India's fast-moving consumer goods (FMCG) landscape.

Established in 2001 and headquartered in Delhi since 2004–05, the company operates across North and East India, working largely with the same distributor partners it onboarded at the outset. This continuity, the company notes, reflects a long-term relationship-driven approach rather than transactional channel management.

"Quality, commitment, and relationships have guided every decision for 24 years," said Girjesh Rungta, Founder and Managing Director. Drawing on his

First published in the Web Edition of Global SME News, globalsmenews.com, available at: https://globalsmenews.com/rungta-tea-marks-24-years-with-92-distributor-retention-outlines-ambitious-expansion/

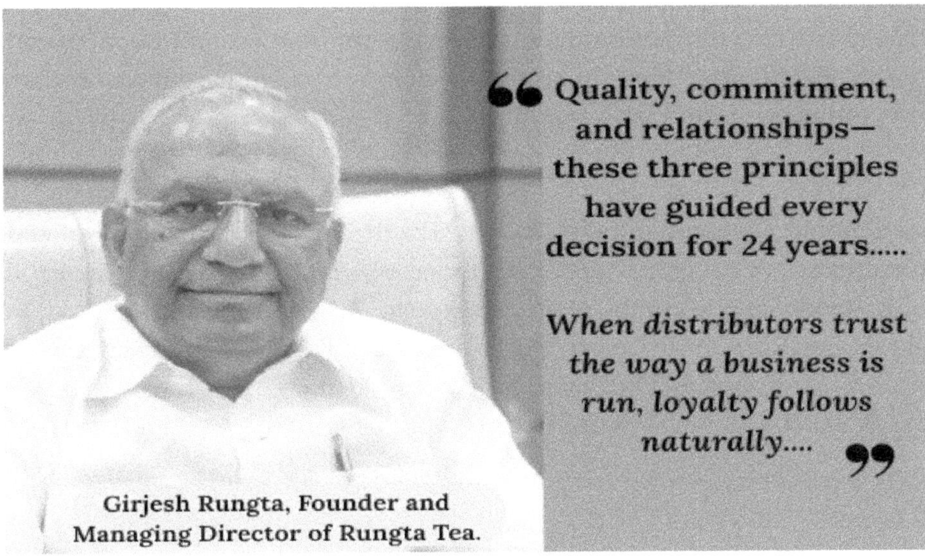

own experience on the distribution side of the business, he emphasized that understanding distributor constraints and incentives has been central to sustaining trust over time.

Rungta Tea is now preparing for a phase of accelerated growth. Over the next two years, the company plans to scale operations at a pace comparable to its cumulative growth over the past two decades. According to management, this ambition is underpinned by infrastructure that has been built with significant headroom.

"Our systems and facilities are designed for a company several times our current size," Mr. Rungta said. "We are not expanding reactively. The capacity is already in place for the next decade."

Manufacturing operations are anchored in Siliguri, where the company maintains close, family-led oversight of quality control. Each year, approximately 2,000 tea samples are evaluated, with only 15–20 ultimately approved for premium product lines. This stringent selection process has helped position the company's flagship Real Gold brand as a consistent performer across multiple regional markets.

Originally rooted in Bihar, Rungta Tea has expanded its footprint to Rajasthan, Uttar Pradesh, Uttarakhand, Jharkhand, and the Delhi NCR. Rajasthan, in particular, has emerged as a strong market for premium blends, reflecting shifting consumer preferences and the company's emphasis on quality differentiation.

Operational transparency is another cornerstone of the firm's model. The company reports that its distributor relationships are built around clear processes and zero-cash transactions, an approach intended to reduce friction and reinforce confidence across the value chain.

"When distributors trust the way a business is run, loyalty follows naturally," Mr. Rungta noted. Founded in 2001, Rungta Tea produces and distributes blended tea products across North and East India. Operating with family-controlled quality standards, the company offers a portfolio that includes Real Gold, Real Gold Classic, Real Gold Select, Real Taste, Real Taste Elaichi Tea, Real Taste Masala Chai, Roz, and Dhamaka. Its current markets span Bihar, Jharkhand, Uttar Pradesh, Uttarakhand, Rajasthan, and Delhi NCR.

What MSMEs need in a fragmenting global economy — lessons from Aninver's fieldwork in entrepreneurship-support programmes

*From Survival to Strategic Resilience***

Jose de la Maza*

In today's fragmenting global economy—where value chains are being reconfigured, financing conditions are tightening, and policy environments evolve at increasing speed—micro, small and medium enterprises (MSMEs) are being asked to do more with less. For many businesses, resilience is no longer a temporary response to disruption; it has become a permanent operating condition that shapes strategy, investment, and day-to-day decision-making.

Drawing on Aninver's experience supporting MSMEs and enterprise ecosystems across multiple regions, one insight emerges consistently: enterprise resilience is rarely built firm-by-firm or in isolation. Instead, it develops when three reinforcing levers are activated simultaneously — capabilities, coordination, and integration. Together, these form the architecture that allows enterprises not merely to survive volatility, but to compete within it.

This article outlines practical lessons from recent programmes — highlighting what worked, what was measured, and what policymakers and ecosystem leaders should prioritise next.

Capabilities that translate into action — not just training attendance

Capability-building is often framed narrowly as "training." Yet resilience stems not from participation, but from behavioural change: stronger financial planning, proactive risk management, diversified markets, and purposeful digital adoption.

*Jose de la Maza. CEO, Aninver Development Partners, an international advisory firm specialised in private sector development, entrepreneurship ecosystems, PPPs, and investment preparation across emerging markets.
**First published in the Web Edition of Global SME News: https://globalsmenews.com/from-survival-to-strategic-resilience-what-msmes-need-in-a-fragmenting-global-economy/

Completion rates and diagnostic engagement therefore matter because they signal whether MSMEs can sustain a learning journey while managing everyday operational pressures.

A structured digital transformation programme in Grenada illustrates this point. The initiative reached 57 SMEs, with 63% completing all mandatory components and a further 21% partially completing them — a meaningful achievement in volatile environments where simply following through is itself a resilience trait. Baseline diagnostics revealed that most participants relied on basic tools such as social media, allocated limited budgets to IT, and prioritised visibility, customer service, and data management. By embedding structured instruments — including a Digital Readiness Assessment, Business Health Survey, and SMART goal-setting — the programme strengthened confidence across critical capability areas.

Key lesson: resilience accelerates when MSMEs are equipped with simple decision frameworks — clear roadmaps, prioritisation tools, and measurable goals — rather than isolated technical content. Practical structure enables strategic thinking.

Coordination as infrastructure: reducing fragmentation and duplication

In many economies, MSME support is not scarce — it is fragmented. Multiple actors implement parallel initiatives, entrepreneurs struggle to navigate the landscape, and institutions often lack the mechanisms to measure system-wide results.

Recent work in The Gambia, funded by the World Bank, identified fragmentation and duplication as core ecosystem weaknesses. Aninver responded by treating coordination not as an administrative function, but as a resilience intervention in its own right.

Ecosystem mapping prioritised three objectives: strengthening the capacity of Enterprise Support Organizations (ESOs), improving national coordination to minimise overlap, and enabling regional integration.

These priorities were operationalised through a collaboration platform featuring a public layer — offering entrepreneurs a directory of services, opportunities, and events — and a secure layer for ESOs that included shared calendars, knowledge libraries, and discussion forums. The intent was explicit: reduce duplication, improve transparency, and support collective learning.

Yet coordination extends beyond digital tools. It requires shared accountability. Standardised monitoring and evaluation instruments, combined with regular reporting requirements, reinforced transparency while enabling system-level insight.

Key lesson: fragmentation is a structural vulnerability; coordination mechanisms are resilience infrastructure.

Integration as strategy in a fragmenting world

Fragmentation is not only global — it is often regional and domestic. Limited connectivity across markets constrains competitiveness, visibility, and investment readiness.

In The Gambia, many ESOs and MSMEs operated in relative isolation from regional networks. The programme therefore positioned regional integration as a strategic pathway to resilience, linking actors to networks, events, and standards that enhance credibility and market access.

Targets included registering ten ESOs with AfriLabs — a pan-African innovation network — by Year 3, alongside facilitating delegations to regional events to build relationships and unlock opportunity.

Key lesson: in uncertain markets, cross-border relationships, recognised standards, and credibility signals become resilience assets — particularly for startups and growth-oriented MSMEs seeking investment or partnerships.

Making resilience measurable

Enterprise programmes frequently over-measure activity while under-measuring outcomes. An ecosystem approach allows for KPI architectures that capture both immediate outputs and longer-term system transformation.

Within WARDIP — a flagship entrepreneurship initiative in The Gambia — the monitoring framework explicitly distinguished short-term results from structural change. Targets included creating 800 jobs by Year 3 and enabling 1,000 MSMEs to access the platform annually, alongside indicators tracking reductions in overlapping activities.

Key lesson: resilience scales when it becomes measurable. Measurement supports adaptive management — not merely retrospective reporting.

Practical digital resilience: what MSMEs actually need

Evidence from tourism-focused MSME programmes in Senegal and Jamaica highlights a pragmatic truth: resilience often begins with foundational improvements. E-commerce readiness, mobile-optimised websites, search engine visibility, digital marketing strategies, and customer management tools frequently deliver the highest immediate returns.

The programmes also demonstrated the value of proportional design. Rather than over-surveying entrepreneurs, teams conducted desk reviews of each firm's online presence to tailor support — balancing analytical rigour with stakeholder fatigue.

Key lesson: the most effective interventions are often lightweight in administrative burden yet precise in diagnosis — starting with a simple question: What is your current posture, and what is the next practical step?

Three policy priorities for 2026

1. Treat MSME resilience as a system, not a collection of isolated trainings.
Support individual firms, but also reform how ESOs coordinate, report, and complement one another.
2. Invest in capability pathways that drive behavioural change.
Diagnostic tools, strategic roadmaps, and measurable goals help enterprises translate learning into better decisions under uncertainty.
3. Build market access through integration.

Regional platforms, shared standards, and credibility networks are not optional extras — they expand opportunity sets when markets fragment.

Aninver's contribution to enterprise resilience lies in bridging capability-building, ecosystem governance, and measurable integration strategies. This approach helps MSMEs move beyond survival mode toward strategic resilience — operating with intent rather than reacting to disruption. Recent experience suggests that the strongest results emerge when practical enterprise tools are combined with system-level coordination and credible pathways to market access.

Strategic Storytelling for Startup/SME Founders

Amit Nagpal, PhD

Strategic storytelling is the intentional use of narrative to achieve specific business or leadership goals. It's about selecting the right story fo the right audience, translating data into meaning and fostering empathy to influence outcomes in areas like branding, change management, sales, fundraising, employer branding and crisis management, making it a powerful tool for leaders.

Here is a founder-friendly taxonomy of strategic stories, followed by practical application areas for business storytelling. This is designed for startup leaders who must sell belief before they sell products.

I. Types of Strategic Stories Startup Founders Can Tell
1. Origin Story
What it does: Establishes authenticity and founder credibility.
Core question answered: Why does this company exist?
Use when: Building trust with early customers, employees, and media.
Signal sent: Purpose precedes profit.

2. Problem Story
What it does: Makes the pain visible and urgent.
Core question: Why must this problem be solved now?
Use when: Pitching investors, onboarding customers.
Signal sent: You understand the market's reality, not just spreadsheets.

3. Vision Story
What it does: Paints a compelling future state.

First published in the Web Edition of Global SME News: globalsmenews.com < https://globalsmenews.com/strategic-storytelling-for-startup-sme-founders/ >

Core question: What does the world look like if we win?
Use when: Fundraising, rallying teams, ecosystem building.
Signal sent: Strategic ambition and long-term thinking.

4. Founder Journey Story
What it does: Humanises leadership.
Core question: Why are you the right person to solve this?
Use when: Personal branding, keynote talks, media interviews.
Signal sent: Resilience, learning velocity, skin in the game.

5. Customer Transformation Story
What it does: Converts features into outcomes.
Core question: What changed for the customer after adoption?
Use when: Sales, case studies, website content.
Signal sent: Measurable value creation.

6. Failure & Pivot Story
What it does: Demonstrates judgment and adaptability.
Core question: What did we learn when things broke?
Use when: Investor conversations, leadership credibility.
Signal sent: Governance maturity and decision discipline.

7. Product Evolution Story
What it does: Explains the logic behind product decisions.
Core question: Why does the product look the way it does today?
Use when: Analysts, partners, enterprise customers.
Signal sent: Strategic coherence, not random iteration.

8. Culture & Values Story
What it does: Attracts aligned talent.
Core question: How do we behave when no one is watching?
Use when: Hiring, internal communication, and employer branding.
Signal sent: Culture is designed, not accidental.

9. Category Creation Story
What it does: Reframes the market itself.
Core question: Why are existing labels inadequate?
Use when: Thought leadership, premium positioning.
Signal sent: Market-shaping intent.

10. Impact & Legacy Story
What it does: Connects business to society.
Core question: Why does this startup matter beyond valuation?
Use when: ESG conversations, policy engagement, global forums.
Signal sent: Long-term relevance and stakeholder awareness.

II. Application Areas for Business Storytelling

1. Fundraising & Investor Relations
Pitch decks
Annual updates
Vision alignment
Outcome: Capital follows clarity.

2. Sales & Customer Acquisition
Discovery calls
Product demos
Objection handling
Outcome: Buyers see themselves in the story.

3. Brand & Marketing
Website narrative
Social media
PR and media interviews
Outcome: Differentiation in noisy markets.

4. Leadership & Internal Alignment
Town halls
Strategy rollouts
Change communication
Outcome: Strategy becomes shared meaning, not slides.

5. Hiring & Employer Branding
Career pages
Interview conversations
Outcome: Values-aligned talent, lower attrition.

6. Partnerships & Ecosystem Building
Strategic alliances
Platform narratives

Outcome: Partners buy into direction, not just deals.

7. Board & Governance Communication
Board decks
Strategic reviews
Risk narratives
Outcome: Better questions, better decisions.

8. Crisis & Reputation Management
Failure disclosures
Public responses
Outcome: Trust retained through transparency.

9. Thought Leadership & Category Authority
Blogs
Keynotes
Whitepapers
Outcome: You define the conversation before competitors do.

10. Scaling & Exit Narratives
IPO story
Acquisition rationale
Outcome: Valuation justified through narrative logic.

A Final Word
Startups fail less because of weak ideas and more because of weak narrative discipline.
Strategy decides what you do. Storytelling decides whether anyone follows.

INDUSTRIALIZATION AT A TURNING POINT

Inclusion, Sustainability, and the Road to 2050

As global industries navigate climate pressures, digital disruption, and structural inequalities, UNIDO's Vision 2050 and Industrial Development Report 2026 set out a renewed case for inclusive, sustainable, and future-ready industrialization. Together, they offer policymakers and industry leaders a data-driven roadmap to ensure the next phase of industrial growth delivers shared prosperity rather than deepening global divides.

At the 21st Session of its General Conference and the Global Industry Summit 2025, United Nations Industrial Development Organization unveiled Vision 2050: The Future of Industries for Development alongside the Industrial Development Report 2026 (IDR26)—a comprehensive agenda aimed at reshaping global industrialization around inclusion, sustainability, and technological transformation.

Announced during a high-level dialogue on "Preparing for the Future of Industrialization," the launch brought together ministers, development partners, private-sector leaders, and leading economists, underscoring the renewed centrality of industrial policy in an era of rapid technological change and demographic transition.

Vision 2050: A New Industrial Deal

UNIDO's Vision 2050 frames industrialization as a primary vehicle for shared prosperity, climate action, and social inclusion. Calling for a global "New Industrial Deal," UNIDO Deputy to the Director General Cecilia Ugaz Estrada emphasized the need for a fairer industrial future where economic growth aligns with decent work, innovation, and environmental stewardship.

The Vision is anchored in four guiding principles:

- Inclusion
- Sustainability
- Resilience
- Innovation-driven development

It outlines a broad set of policy pathways for developing economies, spanning industrial policy support, technology transfer, skills development, quality infrastructure, and clean-energy strategies. The framework is informed by foresight work on digital transformation, future global value chains, and climate and clean-energy transitions.

IDR 2026: Evidence for Policy Choices

Complementing the long-term vision, the Industrial Development Report 2026 provides fresh empirical insights into global industrial performance and the megatrends shaping next-generation production systems.

Key findings indicate that many developing regions remain on the margins of global manufacturing, despite industrialization's central role in achieving the 2030 Agenda. The report highlights the importance of coordinated investments in infrastructure, skills, clean energy, and technology transfer to build future-ready industrial ecosystems.

Scenario-based modelling suggests that expanding agro-industrialization, accelerating clean-energy transitions, and strengthening fairer global value chains could lift millions out of poverty while reducing emissions. Emerging opportunities are identified in clean-tech manufacturing, critical minerals, AI-enabled innovation, and the bioeconomy. At the same time, IDR26 cautions that without deliberate and inclusive policy action, current shifts in technology and trade risk deepening inequalities.

Coordinated Action as the Decisive Factor

Speakers at the launch stressed that realizing Vision 2050 will require unprecedented coordination among governments, development finance institutions, multilateral agencies, and the private sector. A recurring concern was ensuring that green and digital transitions do not amplify existing disparities within and across countries.

UNIDO reaffirmed its commitment to supporting Member States through targeted programmes in industrial and innovation policy design, digital manufacturing and AI adoption, quality infrastructure and standards, sustainable value chain development, skills and capacity-building, and partnerships with regional and global financial institutions. Mobilizing long-term capital for climate-resilient and digitally enabled industries was highlighted as a critical priority.

Shaping the Next Phase of Industrialization

The joint launch of Vision 2050 and IDR26 marks a significant milestone in global industrial policy discourse. By combining a long-term strategic outlook with a strong empirical foundation, UNIDO has positioned industrialization once again at the heart of development thinking—offering governments and industries a practical roadmap to navigate uncertainty and harness emerging opportunities.

The message from Riyadh was clear: with coordinated action, inclusive policies, and sustained investment, a more equitable and sustainable industrial future remains achievable.

In a world marked by fragmentation but sustained interdependence, resilience stems not from size alone, but from smart integration into trade, digital, and regulatory systems.

MSMEs in an Age of Global Fragmentation

By Global SME News Editorial Team

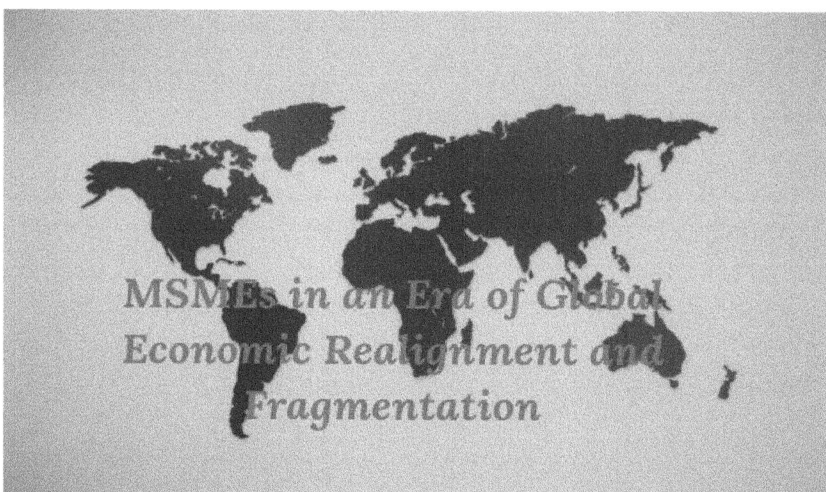

For nearly three decades, MSME policy discourse operated within an expanding framework of trade liberalization, tariff rationalization, multilateral rule-making, and deepening global value chains. Under the umbrella of the World Trade Organization, cross-border commerce became progressively institutionalized, compliance regimes were harmonized, and logistics networks stabilized.

Within that environment, MSMEs were encouraged to integrate into global production networks—often as suppliers, specialized manufacturers, service providers, or export-oriented niche firms. The underlying assumption was policy convergence and regulatory predictability.

The current phase of the global economy reflects a shift—not toward isolation, but toward structured differentiation. Integration persists, yet it is increasingly organized through regional agreements, industrial policy frameworks, digital governance regimes, and strategic trade instruments.

Fragmentation today refers to selective integration across differentiated regulatory and economic blocs.

From Liberalization to Structured Differentiation
The earlier trade architecture emphasized:

- Tariff reduction
- Most-favoured-nation (MFN) treatment

- Expansion of global value chains
- Standardization of customs procedures
- Predictable dispute resolution mechanisms

The present environment reflects increasing complexity:

- Expanded use of trade remedies and safeguard measures
- Active industrial policy and production-linked incentives
- Divergent technical standards and conformity assessments
- Regional trade frameworks such as the Regional Comprehensive Economic Partnership
- Sector-specific digital trade rules

The global system remains interconnected, but not uniformly integrated. Market access is increasingly mediated through regionally embedded trade architectures and differentiated regulatory regimes.

For MSMEs, this alters the operational calculus.

Why MSMEs Face Disproportionate Adjustment Costs

Large multinational enterprises typically diversify market exposure, hedge currency risks, and maintain dedicated regulatory compliance teams. Their scale enables internal absorption of transitional costs arising from regulatory shifts or tariff adjustments.

- MSMEs operate with structural constraints:
- Limited compliance bandwidth
- Restricted access to trade finance
- Concentrated supplier and buyer networks
- Higher exposure to logistics volatility

In an environment of regulatory divergence, MSMEs confront rising transaction costs.

These include:

- Multiple certification requirements
- Rules-of-origin compliance complexity
- Changing tariff classifications
- Digital data compliance mandates
- Payment settlement uncertainties

What was once a relatively standardized export readiness model now demands jurisdiction-specific strategic alignment

MSMEs are transitioning from passive participants in global value chains to active navigators of differentiated trade ecosystems.

Fragmentation as a Multi-Layered Economic Phenomenon

Fragmentation is not confined to tariff policy. It operates across several economic dimensions.

1. Trade Architecture Fragmentation
The proliferation of regional trade agreements alters preferential access patterns. Firms must evaluate tariff schedules, non-tariff measures, and local content rules within specific agreements rather than assume uniform global market conditions.

2. Financial System Fragmentation
Cross-border payment mechanisms, sanctions compliance screening, and currency volatility influence working capital cycles. For MSMEs operating on tight liquidity margins, delayed settlement or exchange-rate fluctuations materially affect viability.

3. Technological and Digital Fragmentation
Divergent data localization requirements, cybersecurity standards, and e-commerce regulations reshape digital trade participation. MSMEs engaged in cross-border services or digital platforms must adapt to multiple compliance environments.

4. Institutional Fragmentation
Variability in enforcement standards, procurement rules, and industrial support policies reduces regulatory predictability. This increases planning uncertainty, particularly for small firms with limited risk-buffer capacity.

Reframing MSME Competitiveness

In a highly liberalized environment, competitiveness was anchored in:

- Cost efficiency
- Integration into global supply chains
- Export scale
- Production specialization

In a differentiated trade order, competitiveness depends increasingly on:

- Regulatory literacy and compliance management
- Regional supply chain embeddedness
- Input diversification strategies
- Digital trade capability
- Trade finance adaptability

The shift is subtle but significant: from pure cost competitiveness to institutional and structural adaptability.

Strategic Implications for MSMEs

Fragmentation redistributes opportunity and risk asymmetrically.

Regional production hubs are strengthening. Industrial policy initiatives are creating domestic supply-chain incentives. Preferential trade agreements offer bloc-based advantages. Digital commerce platforms continue to expand cross-border access—albeit within regulated frameworks.

MSMEs that:

- Align with regional trade corridors
- Invest in certification and standards compliance
- Diversify supplier and market exposure
- Develop internal capacity for regulatory monitoring are likely to identify niche advantages within emerging economic configurations.

Those reliant solely on low-cost production without compliance agility may encounter rising market-entry barriers.

Adaptive Competitiveness in a Differentiated Trade System

The global economy is not contracting; it is reorganizing through layered trade architectures and differentiated regulatory regimes.

For MSMEs, the policy conversation must move beyond export promotion in isolation. It must address trade facilitation, digital compliance capacity, risk diversification, and regionally embedded supply-chain strategies.

In a fragmented yet interconnected world economy, resilience is defined less by scale and more by strategic alignment.

The central question for MSMEs is no longer whether global integration is possible—but how to operate competitively within multiple, overlapping trade systems.

Trade Realignment and the Future of Small Enterprise Participation

As global trade systems recalibrate around new standards and shifting supply chains, small enterprises face rising compliance demands and financial pressures. Trade realignment is reshaping the conditions of MSME participation and redefining the parameters of their future competitiveness.

Trade Realignment and the Future of Small Enterprise Participation

By Global SME News Editorial Team

For nearly three decades, small enterprises were encouraged to internationalize. Export promotion programmes, digital platforms, and global value chains reduced entry barriers and expanded market access. By 2022, global merchandise trade had reached approximately USD 25 trillion, according to data from the World Trade Organization. Yet beneath this aggregate expansion, the operating environment has become more complex, differentiated, and compliance-intensive.

Recent years have witnessed a steady increase in trade restrictions, technology controls, and regulatory divergence across major markets. The WTO's monitoring reports indicate a rising stock of trade-restrictive measures since 2018. Simultaneously, export control regimes in advanced economies have expanded to cover advanced semiconductors, critical minerals, and dual-use technologies. For large multinational firms, these developments are absorbed through dedicated compliance departments. For micro, small and medium enterprises (MSMEs), they alter the structural conditions of participation.

Human Capital: Compliance as Core Capability

MSMEs typically operate with lean management structures. Owners and small teams oversee operations, marketing, finance, and regulatory documentation. In such systems, specialization is limited. However, fragmented regulatory systems demand a new layer of competence: trade compliance literacy, cross-border taxation knowledge, digital governance awareness, and continuous risk monitoring across markets.

Export transactions increasingly require detailed classification under harmonized tariff systems, adherence to rules of origin under Free Trade Agreements, and verification against sanctions lists. According to surveys conducted by the International Trade Centre, smaller firms report significantly higher compliance costs relative to turnover compared to large enterprises. Fixed advisory expenses do not scale down with firm size.

Human capital, therefore, is being redefined. It is no longer sufficient to focus solely on production efficiency. Regulatory intelligence—the capacity to interpret evolving compliance frameworks—has become integral to competitiveness. In practice, many MSMEs struggle to internalize this shift due to cost constraints and limited access to specialized advisory ecosystems.

Digital Compliance and Divergent Standards

Digital trade has expanded rapidly. Cross-border e-commerce sales exceeded USD 5 trillion globally in recent years, with projections continuing upward. Yet digital connectivity increasingly operates within differentiated regulatory systems.

More than 100 countries now maintain data protection or privacy legislation. Several jurisdictions have introduced data localization requirements, compelling firms to store or process certain categories of data domestically. Compliance with frameworks such as the EU's General Data Protection Regulation has extraterritorial implications for firms exporting digital services.

Cybersecurity has become another threshold requirement. Supplier integration with multinational corporations often requires certification under recognized standards such as ISO/IEC 27001. For MSMEs, certification audits and system upgrades represent fixed investments that compete with working capital. Platform dependency further complicates the landscape; algorithmic policy changes by dominant digital intermediaries can alter market visibility without prior negotiation.

Digital fragmentation thus increases transaction costs in a manner that is disproportionately burdensome for smaller enterprises. Connectivity now carries regulatory conditions.

Financial Pressures in an Uncertain Trade Environment

Access to finance has historically constrained MSME growth. The International Finance Corporation estimates the global MSME financing gap at over USD 5 trillion annually in emerging markets alone. In a context marked by heightened policy uncertainty and currency volatility, these gaps widen.

Banks reassess risk exposure across certain corridors, particularly where sanctions or regulatory shifts affect settlement systems. Trade finance becomes more selective, and risk premiums rise. The International Monetary Fund has cautioned that fragmentation in trade and financial systems could reduce global output over the medium term. The World Bank has similarly noted that capital efficiency may decline as supply chains reconfigure.

For MSMEs, these macroeconomic signals translate into tighter credit conditions, higher hedging costs, and greater exposure to exchange-rate fluctuations. Unlike large corporations, small firms rarely deploy structured hedging instruments. Import-dependent enterprises, particularly in manufacturing and processing sectors, experience direct margin compression when currencies depreciate.

Supply Chain Realignment and Entry Barriers

Global supply chains are undergoing recalibration toward reliability, resilience, and regulatory compliance. According to recent industry analyses, multinational firms have increased supplier diversification initiatives since 2020 to mitigate concentration risks.

For MSMEs, this restructuring has mixed implications. Higher environmental, social, and governance (ESG) reporting standards, traceability requirements, and cybersecurity audits may raise entry thresholds. Certification costs can delay or deter participation in strategic sectors such as electronics, pharmaceuticals, and renewable energy components.

At the same time, diversification strategies open selective opportunities for regionally embedded firms capable of rapid adaptation. As firms reduce over-concentration in single markets, smaller suppliers positioned within stable trade arrangements may benefit from new procurement pathways. Outcomes depend heavily on domestic institutional support and the speed at which MSMEs can align with upgraded standards.

Policy Architecture: Bridging the Domestic-Global Gap

A structural mismatch persists between domestic MSME policies and transnational operational realities. Credit guarantee schemes, entrepreneurship promotion initiatives, and cluster development programmes often do not incorporate trade advisory support, digital compliance training, or real-time market intelligence.

Free Trade Agreements frequently remain underutilized by smaller firms due to limited awareness of rules of origin and documentation procedures. Export advisory ecosystems in many countries remain underdeveloped relative to the complexity of contemporary trade frameworks.

Fragmentation requires integrated policy ecosystems that connect trade facilitation, digital infrastructure governance, financial resilience instruments, and industrial upgrading. Without such integration, MSMEs face layered regulatory systems with fragmented institutional guidance.

A Structural Transition

The global economy is not retreating from cross-border exchange, but it is operating through more differentiated and compliance-intensive channels. Market access increasingly depends on regulatory alignment, digital readiness, and financial resilience.

For MSMEs, this represents a structural transition rather than a cyclical disruption. Competitive survival now requires the capacity to interpret regulatory frameworks, absorb compliance costs, and manage volatility without scale advantages. Whether inclusive global commerce can be sustained will depend not only on entrepreneurial adaptability, but on whether institutional systems evolve to match the complexity of the emerging trade and regulatory landscape.

SME policy must move beyond traditional credit and cluster models toward a capability-centred framework that integrates digital infrastructure, knowledge upgrading, and institutional coherence. In a knowledge-driven economy, competitiveness depends not merely on access to capital, but on integration into digital, trade, and innovation systems.

Beyond Credit and Clusters

Why SME Policy Must Enter the Capability Era

Perumal Koshy

For more than three decades, small-enterprise policy across much of the world has revolved around two familiar instruments: expanding access to credit and building industrial clusters. The rationale was rooted in industrial-era economics. Capital was scarce, proximity generated scale efficiencies, and productivity gains flowed from machinery, logistics, and spatial concentration.

This policy architecture shaped development finance institutions, export processing zones, credit guarantee schemes, and subsidised industrial estates. It delivered measurable gains in manufacturing output and employment generation. Yet it was designed for an economic structure in which tangible assets defined competitiveness. That structure has changed.

The Knowledge Economy Shift

The contemporary global economy is increasingly organised around data flows, digital platforms, intangible assets, and knowledge-intensive services. Digitally delivered services now constitute a growing share of global trade. Cross-border commerce is mediated not only through ports and industrial corridors, but through

platforms, cloud systems, and interoperable digital infrastructures.
In such an environment, the constraint facing small and medium enterprises (SMEs) is no longer solely capital scarcity. It is integration capacity.
SMEs account for the overwhelming majority of firms globally and provide more than half of total employment. Their macroeconomic significance is beyond dispute. The question is whether policy frameworks designed for physical production systems remain adequate in an economy where value is increasingly generated through connectivity, information, and adaptive capability.

A loan may finance equipment. It does not automatically generate digital competence. A cluster may reduce transport costs. It does not ensure algorithmic visibility on a global platform.

From Factor Support to Capability Systems

Traditional SME promotion operated on a factor-accumulation model: provide finance, improve infrastructure, reduce regulatory burdens. In the knowledge economy, competitiveness depends less on factor inputs and more on systemic capabilities—institutions, digital networks, regulatory coherence, technological literacy, and organisational adaptability.

This implies a theoretical shift: from factor-based support to capability-based competitiveness.

Capability, in this sense, refers to a firm's ability to integrate into digital trade networks, comply with evolving standards, manage data securely, and navigate platform-based market structures. It is not merely about possessing assets; it is about deploying them within interconnected systems.

SME policy, therefore, must evolve from isolated instruments toward a capability-oriented state architecture—one that actively constructs the institutional conditions for digital participation.

Digital Public Infrastructure as Economic Architecture

Digital public infrastructure has emerged as a foundational layer of enterprise integration. Interoperable e-invoicing systems, electronic customs windows, digital identity frameworks, and integrated tax platforms reduce transaction costs while generating verifiable data trails.

These systems do more than enhance administrative efficiency. They formalise enterprise participation and reduce informational asymmetries that historically excluded smaller firms from formal finance and export markets. When tax systems connect with banking databases and digital payment platforms, they create visibility. Visibility improves creditworthiness. Creditworthiness expands opportunity.

In this model, digital governance tools become economic infrastructure.
The experience of countries that have invested in unified digital tax and compliance systems illustrates this transformation. Enterprises become part of an integrated economic circuit rather than operating at the margins of formal systems.

The Competence Gap

Yet infrastructure alone does not produce competitiveness. Digitalisation yields productivity gains only when firms develop the capabilities to use digital tools strategically.

Many SMEs have adopted basic digital interfaces—websites, social media pages, online listings. Fewer possess data analytics capacity, platform optimisation knowledge, cross-border digital compliance skills, or intellectual property awareness in knowledge markets.

The gap, therefore, is not access but competence.

Targeted capability upgrading—data literacy, digital marketing strategy, platform governance understanding, cybersecurity hygiene, and standards adaptation—is increasingly central to SME competitiveness. Generic training programmes are insufficient. The knowledge economy demands specialised skill formation aligned with digital market structures.

Trade in the Age of Platforms

Trade itself is undergoing structural change. Digitally delivered services—consulting, design, education, business services—are increasingly transacted across borders through digital channels. International datasets now track these flows across hundreds of economies.

Regional initiatives that digitise customs procedures and harmonise electronic documentation demonstrate how institutional integration lowers entry barriers for smaller firms. Where trade facilitation becomes digital and interoperable, participation expands. Where it remains paper-based and fragmented, smaller enterprises face disproportionate friction.

In effect, digital trade facilitation compresses distance. SMEs no longer require physical presence to access foreign markets; they require digital visibility and compliance readiness.

The New Vulnerabilities: Cyber and Sustainability

Integration into digital networks also introduces new risks. SMEs frequently operate with limited cybersecurity preparedness despite facing comparable threat environments to larger corporations. A single cyber incident can halt operations, compromise client data, and damage reputation irreversibly.

Cybersecurity thus becomes a structural policy issue rather than a discretionary technical upgrade. Shared advisory services, subsidised audits, and coordinated resilience frameworks must form part of mainstream SME promotion.

Simultaneously, global value chains are embedding sustainability compliance and environmental traceability into procurement standards. Digital systems enable traceability and reporting, but only for firms capable of generating reliable data. As environmental standards tighten, exclusion risks will fall disproportionately on firms lacking digital and compliance capacity.

Digital capability and sustainability compliance are converging dimensions of competitiveness.

Reimagining Policy Architecture

What emerges is the need for an integrated policy architecture. Credit instruments and cluster development remain relevant, but they must operate within a broader ecosystem that integrates:

- Digital public infrastructure
- Specialised capability upgrading
- Platform and trade facilitation integration
- Cybersecurity resilience
- Sustainability enablement

This requires coordination across finance ministries, digital economy authorities, trade departments, and innovation agencies. Institutional silos weaken outcomes. The knowledge economy rewards policy coherence.

The deeper philosophical shift is from viewing SMEs as passive recipients of support toward recognising them as nodes within interconnected economic systems. Competitiveness arises from embeddedness—within data networks, regulatory frameworks, platform ecosystems, and innovation circuits.

The Capability Imperative

SMEs will continue to anchor employment, diversification, and social inclusion. Yet in an economy defined increasingly by intangible flows rather than physical throughput, capital provision alone cannot secure long-term competitiveness. The credit era built enterprises. The capability era must connect them.

Policy must therefore move beyond expanding finance toward constructing the institutional and digital capabilities that enable SMEs to participate meaningfully in evolving regional and global economic networks. Without such recalibration, traditional support instruments risk reinforcing structural vulnerability rather than resilience.

The transition from credit to capability is not a marginal adjustment. It is the defining task of SME policy in the digital age.

Artificial intelligence is reshaping how work is performed, but it is not erasing the sectors that anchor economic demand. Healthcare, education, renewable energy, infrastructure, sustainable agriculture, tourism, creative industries, environmental services, and community-based enterprises are positioned for continued expansion as technology modernizes delivery systems rather than eliminating them. The employment shift underway is structural reallocation within sectors, not sectoral extinction.

Beyond Automation: Why Employment Will Expand as AI Modernizes Core Sectors

Jenna Carol

The global debate on artificial intelligence frequently reduces the future of work to displacement scenarios. Evidence from long cycles of technological change suggests a more precise interpretation. Automation reorganizes tasks within sectors; it rarely eliminates sectors where demand is anchored in demographics, infrastructure deficits, ecological transition, or essential consumption. AI substitutes routine components of production. It does not eliminate the need for care, food systems, energy deployment, education, infrastructure, or localized services.

Assessments from the International Labour Organization indicate that exposure to automation is concentrated in clerical and repetitive administrative roles. At the same time, expansion is projected in health services, green industries, infrastructure-linked occupations, and skills development. The World Economic Forum similarly identifies renewable energy, care services, vocational education, and sustainability-related activities among the fastest-growing employment domains. The pattern is reallocation within sectors rather than sectoral extinction.

The employment frontiers most likely to expand over the coming decade include: Healthcare and Long-Term Care Services

Ageing populations and rising chronic disease burdens create sustained service demand. The World Health Organization projects a global shortfall of nearly 10 million health workers by 2030. AI-enabled diagnostics and robotic systems enhance productivity, yet nursing, geriatric assistance, rehabilitation, mental health services, and home-based care remain human-intensive.

Education, Technical Training, and Lifelong Learning

Technological transition drives continuous reskilling. Adaptive platforms and AI-based assessment tools expand access, but vocational instruction, mentoring, and institutional governance remain labor-centered. Technical institutes and applied skills academies show strong growth potential.

Renewable Energy and Energy Transition Services

Renewable energy employment has surpassed 13 million jobs globally, according to the International Renewable Energy Agency. Installation, grid modernization, storage deployment, and system maintenance remain labor-absorbing even as robotics enhances manufacturing efficiency. Climate commitments under the United Nations Framework Convention on Climate Change continue to accelerate investment flows.

The Broader Care Economy

Childcare, disability services, elderly companionship, and community-based social work expand alongside urbanization and rising workforce participation. Evidence from the Organisation for Economic Co-operation and Development shows that care investments generate high employment multipliers. Digital coordination tools support delivery without replacing human interaction.

Infrastructure Development and Urban Resilience

Transport, sanitation, water systems, housing, and climate-resilient infrastructure require sustained investment through 2040. Automation enhances surveying and project management, yet on-site execution, retrofitting, compliance, and maintenance remain employment-intensive.

Sustainable Agriculture and Agri-Processing

Food demand continues to rise. The Food and Agriculture Organization projects ongoing increases in output requirements. Precision technologies raise productivity, while employment shifts toward processing, certification, cold-chain logistics, advisory services, and value-added food systems.

Tourism, Hospitality, and Experiential Services
Cultural tourism, eco-lodges, wellness retreats, and heritage services depend on physical experience and localized authenticity. Digital systems optimize bookings, but service delivery remains human-centered.

Creative Industries and Cultural Production
Generative AI alters workflows, yet storytelling, live performance, gaming design, brand identity development, and artisanal production continue to rely on human creativity. Hybrid human–AI production models are likely to expand sectoral output.

Environmental Management and Circular Economy Services
Recycling systems, refurbishment networks, environmental auditing, and sustainability compliance services expand under tightening regulatory frameworks. Automation supports sorting systems, but localized collection and repair ecosystems sustain employment.

Personal and Community-Based Micro Enterprises
Proximity-based services such as repair, tailoring, catering, wellness, and neighborhood retail remain resistant to full automation due to their physical and relational nature. Digital platforms enhance coordination and payments without replacing the service interface.

Across these sectors, three durable drivers sustain employment expansion. Demographic momentum increases demand for health, education, and care. Climate and energy transitions require large-scale deployment of new systems. Human-centered interaction—trust, contextual judgment, ethical discretion—remains beyond full automation. AI and robotics modernize delivery systems, reduce routine task intensity, and create complementary roles in oversight, maintenance, data interpretation, and compliance management.

Employment will evolve in composition and skill requirements. The sectors themselves will endure and, in many cases, expand.

As digital payment systems become core economic infrastructure, small enterprises are gaining faster liquidity, expanded market access, and data-driven credit opportunities—while facing rising cybersecurity risks, compliance burdens, and regulatory fragmentation. This feature examines the structural implications of digital payments for SMEs and consumers, and evaluates how evolving international policy frameworks are shaping the future of secure, inclusive financial ecosystems.

Digital Payments and the Small Enterprise Economy

Security Architecture, Policy Frameworks, and the Restructuring of Market Access

Mc Bride

Digital payment systems have evolved into foundational economic infrastructure shaping enterprise competitiveness, liquidity management, and financial inclusion. For micro and small enterprises, payment architecture determines how quickly revenues are realized, how transparently transactions are recorded, and how effectively firms integrate into formal financial systems. For consumers, digital payments redefine access, convenience, and exposure to new forms of financial and technological risk. The World Bank's Global Findex Database (2021) indicates that 76% of adults globally now possess a financial account, compared to 51% in 2011, with mobile-enabled systems driving much of this expansion. Simultaneously, the Bank for International Settlements reports that the majority of central banks now operate or support fast payment systems, embedding instant settlement capabilities into national economic frameworks. Yet numerical expansion in access does not automatically translate into resilience, productive integration, or security for small enterprises operating within thin-margin sectors.

Digital payments function not merely as transactional instruments but as working capital infrastructure. For MSMEs, especially in retail, logistics, and service-oriented sectors, faster settlement cycles improve cash-flow predictability and reduce reliance on informal borrowing channels. India's Unified Payments Interface (UPI), developed by the National Payments Corporation of India under regulatory oversight of the Reserve Bank of India, demonstrates how interoperable, low-cost payment rails can transform retail ecosystems. Transaction volumes crossing 100 billion annually indicate both scale efficiency and public trust in digital public infrastructure. Similar systems—Brazil's Pix, Singapore's PayNow, and the UK's Faster Payments—illustrate a broader structural shift toward instant, interoperable domestic payment architecture. For small merchants, these systems reduce cash-handling risk, lower transaction friction, and create digital transaction histories that enhance financial visibility.

Beyond liquidity efficiency, digital payments generate data trails that increasingly influence credit access. The global SME finance gap remains substantial, with estimates from the World Bank and the International Finance Corporation placing unmet financing demand at over USD 5 trillion annually. Fintech lenders now leverage payment transaction data to construct alternative credit scoring models, partially addressing information asymmetry that traditionally excluded informal or collateral-light enterprises from formal lending systems. Revenue-based lending, invoice discounting platforms, and embedded finance solutions are expanding across multiple jurisdictions. However, reliance on algorithmic credit scoring introduces new structural concerns, including opacity in risk modelling, potential discrimination embedded within datasets, and limited avenues for appeal or correction.

For consumers, digital payments expand convenience and formal financial participation, especially in environments where welfare transfers, remittances, and subsidies are digitally routed. However, embedded credit features within payment applications may accelerate consumer indebtedness, particularly where financial literacy levels are uneven. Additionally, the proliferation of digital wallets and app-based ecosystems increases exposure to phishing attacks, SIM-swap fraud, and social engineering scams. National cyber emergency response teams across several regions report that small businesses and individual consumers constitute a significant proportion of reported digital fraud cases, often due to inadequate multi-factor authentication practices or limited cybersecurity awareness.

Security architecture has therefore become central to payment system stability. Small enterprises frequently lack dedicated IT governance structures, rendering them vulnerable to ransomware attacks and payment gateway breaches. Real-time settlement systems, while efficient, compress fraud detection windows, increasing the speed at which financial losses can materialize. Insurance coverage for cyber incidents remains underdeveloped in many jurisdictions, and small enterprises often operate without structured incident response protocols. Data governance concerns further complicate the ecosystem. Payment systems generate extensive transaction metadata, raising questions regarding ownership, portability, monetization rights, and liability in the event of breaches. The European Union's GDPR framework, alongside emerging digital personal data protection regimes in Asia and Africa, attempts to define responsibilities, but enforcement capacity and cross-border interoperability remain uneven.

At the international level, regulatory responses reflect attempts to balance innovation with systemic stability. Regulatory sandboxes have been adopted by central banks in numerous jurisdictions to test fintech innovations under supervised conditions. Open banking frameworks, including the European Union's PSD2 directive, promote API-based data sharing to enhance competition while limiting monopolistic platform dominance. Cross-border payment reform initiatives under the G20 aim to reduce remittance costs and improve settlement efficiency, yet progress remains fragmented due to divergent compliance standards, foreign exchange controls, and anti-money laundering frameworks.

Central bank digital currency (CBDC) exploration represents another dimension of policy experimentation. More than one hundred central banks are evaluating or piloting CBDC models, considering retail architectures that could reshape SME payment ecosystems. Proponents argue that CBDCs could enhance settlement efficiency, reduce remittance costs, and increase traceability in combating illicit finance. Critics highlight potential disintermediation risks for commercial banks, privacy trade-offs, and operational resilience challenges. The long-term implications for small enterprise liquidity and banking relationships remain uncertain.

Despite technological advances, structural constraints persist for SMEs. Merchant discount rates in card-based systems continue to affect profitability in low-margin sectors. Compliance costs associated with anti-money laundering and know-your-customer requirements disproportionately burden micro-enterprises. Technology acquisition expenses, digital literacy gaps, and ongoing cybersecurity investment requirements create barriers to optimal adoption. Furthermore, fragmented cross-border interoperability limits small exporters' ability to seamlessly integrate into global e-commerce ecosystems.

Policy frameworks must therefore move beyond innovation narratives toward inclusive regulatory architecture. Tiered compliance mechanisms for micro-enterprises, subsidized cybersecurity capacity-building programs, interoperable fast payment networks, and clearly defined liability frameworks between banks, fintech providers, and merchants are essential components of a resilient ecosystem. Consumer protection tribunals for digital fraud redress and standardized dispute resolution mechanisms can enhance trust without suppressing innovation.

Digital payment systems now operate as economic governance infrastructure rather than peripheral financial utilities. For small enterprises, they offer measurable advantages in liquidity management, market access, and credit visibility. For consumers, they expand participation while introducing new categories of technological risk. The future competitiveness of the small enterprise sector will depend not solely on digital adoption rates but on the robustness, transparency, and equity of the institutional frameworks governing payment ecosystems across jurisdictions. In the evolving global financial architecture, payment systems are not simply channels of exchange; they are determinants of economic inclusion, resilience, and systemic stability.

As small enterprises expand their use of cloud platforms, digital payments, and data-driven systems, exposure to operational and financial risk increases. Evolving threat patterns, enterprise protection frameworks, market solutions, and regulatory responses are reshaping how SMEs manage resilience in an increasingly interconnected digital economy.

Securing the Digital Enterprise

Strategic Risk Management, Technological Pathways, and Emerging Innovation in the SME Ecosystem

Svetlana M

The contemporary small enterprise operates within an interconnected digital environment shaped by cloud computing, online payments, e-commerce platforms, remote collaboration tools, and data-driven decision systems. This connectivity enhances productivity and market reach, yet it simultaneously expands exposure to malicious intrusion, operational disruption, and reputational risk. For small and medium enterprises (SMEs), the question is no longer whether they will face digital threats, but whether they possess the institutional capacity to anticipate, withstand, and recover from them.

Global estimates suggest that cyber-related economic losses now run into trillions of dollars annually, with smaller firms disproportionately affected due to limited internal safeguards and fragmented response systems. In supply-chain structures, SMEs are frequently targeted as access points to larger enterprises. The issue therefore extends beyond individual firms to the stability of entire value chains. For a sector that contributes more than 90% of businesses worldwide and over half of global employment, resilience in the digital domain has become a macroeconomic concern.

From Technical Safeguards to Enterprise Risk Architecture

Digital protection is often misunderstood as a purely technical matter confined to software tools. In practice, it is an integrated risk management function embedded within governance, compliance, financial oversight, and operational continuity planning. At its foundation lies the protection of information assets—ensuring that data remains confidential, accurate, and accessible when required. When these three pillars are compromised, the enterprise faces financial losses, contractual disputes, and erosion of stakeholder trust.

Modern threat vectors increasingly exploit behavioural vulnerabilities rather than system flaws. Deceptive communication tactics, identity spoofing, credential harvesting, and manipulated digital content are now common methods of intrusion. Smaller firms, often lacking structured internal controls, are particularly vulnerable to such tactics. Consequently, resilience depends not only on infrastructure but also on employee awareness and leadership commitment.

Evolving Strategic Models

The conventional model of defending a defined network perimeter has diminished in relevance. Remote work, mobile access, and cloud platforms dissolve fixed boundaries. Contemporary enterprise protection strategies therefore emphasize continuous verification of identity and activity rather than presumed trust based on location. This "trust nothing, verify everything" model reduces internal lateral movement during breaches and limits systemic exposure.

Layered defense models remain critical. By integrating multiple safeguards—network monitoring, device-level protection, encrypted communication channels, and anomaly detection—enterprises create redundancy that absorbs shocks when individual controls fail. For SMEs, modular adoption of such layered structures offers a pragmatic balance between cost and coverage.

Risk-prioritisation frameworks also guide resource allocation. Rather than seeking absolute immunity from threats, firms evaluate vulnerabilities according to likelihood and impact. International standards bodies and regulatory agencies increasingly encourage structured risk assessment methodologies, linking digital resilience with corporate governance obligations. This shift has regulatory implications, as compliance requirements are progressively extending to smaller enterprises operating within critical supply networks.

Market Instruments and Technology Ecosystems

The global market for enterprise protection solutions has expanded rapidly, driven by cloud migration and digitised operations. Tools can be grouped into several functional categories relevant to SMEs.

Device-level protection platforms safeguard laptops, servers, and mobile equipment against malicious software and unauthorised access. Advanced versions employ behavioural analytics to detect abnormal activity patterns.

Integrated monitoring systems consolidate signals from devices, networks, and applications into unified dashboards, enabling rapid identification of irregular behaviour. Subscription-based monitoring services are increasingly attractive to SMEs that lack in-house specialists.

Identity management systems regulate access privileges, reducing the risk of credential misuse. Multi-factor authentication and biometric verification are now baseline requirements rather than optional add-ons.

Cloud-native safeguards ensure that data stored offsite remains encrypted and compliant with data protection standards. Misconfiguration of cloud environments is a frequent source of breaches; automated compliance checks therefore play a preventive role.

Insurance products tailored to digital risk are gaining traction, transferring portions of financial exposure. However, insurers often require demonstrable preventive measures before underwriting coverage, effectively reinforcing adoption of baseline safeguards.

Innovation Pathways Reshaping Enterprise Protection

Technological advancement is reshaping defensive capabilities. Machine-learning algorithms can now detect behavioural anomalies in real time, identifying suspicious login patterns, irregular data flows, or unusual network traffic. While such tools enhance responsiveness, adversaries are simultaneously deploying artificial intelligence to automate deception campaigns, creating a dynamic contest between defensive and offensive innovation.

Converged networking and protection architectures delivered via cloud platforms enable secure connectivity for distributed workforces. These models integrate traffic management and threat monitoring into unified service layers, reducing complexity for smaller firms.

Distributed ledger technologies are being explored to strengthen transaction integrity within supply chains, enhancing traceability and reducing fraud. Though not universally applicable, such approaches may become relevant in sectors requiring high levels of contractual transparency.

Hardware-level safeguards embedded directly into devices offer additional protection against firmware manipulation and low-level attacks. For SMEs procuring new equipment, built-in security modules can provide cost-effective resilience.

Privacy-enhancing computation techniques allow sensitive data to be analysed without direct exposure, enabling compliance with increasingly stringent data protection regimes while preserving analytic capabilities. This innovation is particularly relevant in sectors where customer data forms the basis of competitive advantage.

Structural Constraints Facing Smaller Firms

Despite technological progress, structural limitations persist. Budgetary constraints frequently delay proactive investment. Skilled professionals in enterprise protection remain scarce and costly. Fragmented vendor ecosystems create interoperability challenges. Moreover, regulatory obligations often apply uniformly across enterprise sizes, generating disproportionate compliance burdens for micro-enterprises.

There is also a cultural dimension. Many smaller firms perceive digital safeguards as reactive expenditures rather than strategic investments. Yet operational downtime following a breach can disrupt revenue cycles, undermine contractual commitments, and trigger reputational damage that exceeds immediate financial losses.

Governance and Policy Context

Public authorities increasingly recognise digital resilience as a component of economic security. Legislative frameworks in Europe, North America, and Asia now impose clearer obligations regarding incident reporting, risk assessment, and data protection. Capacity-building initiatives, awareness campaigns, and co-financed training programs aim to enhance preparedness within the SME segment.

A balanced regulatory architecture should incorporate proportionate compliance thresholds, financial incentives for preventive investment, and streamlined reporting procedures. Cross-border cooperation is equally critical, given the transnational nature of digital threats. Information-sharing platforms between public agencies and private enterprises can significantly reduce response times during large-scale incidents.

Toward Embedded Resilience

The digital transformation of commerce has integrated technology into every layer of enterprise activity—payments, logistics, procurement, marketing, and customer engagement. In such an environment, resilience in the digital sphere is inseparable from overall business continuity. For SMEs, building this resilience requires more than software acquisition; it demands leadership awareness, structured governance, employee training, and integration of risk management into strategic planning.

The competitive landscape of 2026 and beyond will reward enterprises that treat digital protection not as an afterthought but as embedded infrastructure. As global markets become increasingly interconnected and compliance frameworks tighten, the capacity of small enterprises to safeguard their digital assets will influence not only individual firm survival but also the credibility and stability of broader economic systems

As Artificial Intelligence moves from experimentation to everyday business application, small enterprises face a defining moment. For some, AI-driven tools are unlocking productivity gains, sharper market insights, and leaner operations. For others, limited digital readiness, financial constraints, and skill gaps risk widening competitive disparities. The future of AI in the SME sector will depend not only on technological access, but on whether ecosystems can ensure inclusive and equitable adoption.

AI Adoption in Small Enterprises: Productivity Tool or New Divide?

Chris Peterson

Artificial Intelligence is no longer a speculative frontier reserved for technology conglomerates; it is steadily embedding itself into the operational architecture of small enterprises. From AI-enabled accounting systems and demand forecasting tools to chatbots, automated marketing platforms, and generative design applications, digital intelligence is reshaping how small firms manage time, cost, and market engagement. What distinguishes the current phase is accessibility. Cloud-based subscription models and Software-as-a-Service (SaaS) platforms have lowered entry barriers, allowing even micro-enterprises to experiment with AI-driven efficiencies.

For digitally prepared SMEs, AI functions as a productivity multiplier. Automated invoicing reduces administrative overhead. Predictive analytics improves inventory turnover and working capital management. Customer data analysis refines market segmentation and enhances retention strategies. In export-linked enterprises, AI tools assist with documentation, regulatory tracking, and demand projections across geographies. The cumulative effect is operational compression—more output per unit of labour and capital. For small firms operating on thin margins, even incremental efficiency gains can significantly improve resilience.

At a macro level, AI adoption among SMEs aligns with broader digital transformation agendas pursued across advanced and emerging economies. As supply chains become data-driven and compliance frameworks more technology-intensive, enterprises capable of integrating AI into core processes are better positioned to participate in formal value chains. In sectors such as retail, logistics, fintech services, light manufacturing, and digital commerce, AI is increasingly intertwined with competitiveness.

Yet, the diffusion of AI across the SME landscape is uneven. A structural divide persists between enterprises that possess digital readiness—stable internet connectivity, trained personnel, financial buffers for experimentation—and those operating within resource-constrained environments. Micro-enterprises in informal markets, traditional craft clusters, or rural production networks often face layered constraints: limited access to affordable digital infrastructure, low digital literacy, and uncertainty around cybersecurity and data governance. For many, foundational digitization—basic accounting software, e-commerce onboarding, or digital payments—remains incomplete. Advanced AI integration, therefore, risks becoming a second-order privilege.

Cost structures also matter. While AI tools are marketed as affordable, cumulative subscription fees, integration expenses, and training investments can become burdensome for enterprises with volatile cash flows. Moreover, AI systems require reliable data inputs; enterprises with fragmented record-keeping or informal transaction practices may struggle to generate usable datasets. Without deliberate ecosystem support, early adopters could accelerate ahead, consolidating productivity and market access, while others remain locked into low-technology equilibria.

The central concern is not technological inevitability but distributional impact. If AI adoption becomes concentrated among digitally mature SMEs, the sector itself may fragment into tiers of productivity and competitiveness. This internal stratification could deepen inequalities within local business ecosystems, particularly where small enterprises are primary sources of employment and community-level economic stability.

Ensuring that AI operates as an inclusive productivity instrument requires coordinated interventions. Affordable digital financing mechanisms, sector-specific AI toolkits, localized training modules, shared technology hubs, and strengthened digital public infrastructure are critical. Enterprise development institutions, industry associations, and financial intermediaries must shift from generic digital advocacy to practical, use-case driven support models tailored to micro and small enterprises.

Artificial Intelligence holds undeniable promise for efficiency, innovation, and scalability within the SME sector. Whether it becomes a bridge to enhanced productivity or a catalyst for a new digital divide will depend on how ecosystems align technological advancement with inclusion. The trajectory remains open—but policy, finance, and institutional design will determine which path prevails.

Women-led enterprises are expanding across sectors, yet their presence in export markets remains disproportionately low. Certification burdens, logistics asymmetries, digital platform governance, and fragmented trade facilitation systems continue to shape uneven access to global value chains. Addressing these structural frictions is central to unlocking sustained export participation and competitiveness for women-led SMEs.

Women-Led Enterprises in Export Markets

Structural Barriers and Emerging Platforms

Svetlana M

Women-led enterprises are expanding across sectors ranging from agro-processing and textiles to digital services, wellness products, and creative industries. Domestic participation rates have risen steadily in many emerging and transition economies. Yet cross-border trade participation remains disproportionately low. The gap is not simply a function of entrepreneurial capability. It reflects structural constraints embedded in export certification regimes, logistics systems, digital marketplace governance, and institutional trade frameworks.

Data from the World Trade Organization and the International Trade Centre consistently show that women-owned or women-led firms export at lower rates than their male-led counterparts, particularly in manufacturing and higher value-added services. The asymmetry is systemic rather than incidental.

Certification as a Gatekeeping Mechanism

For small enterprises entering export markets, compliance is not incremental; it is foundational. Quality standards, sanitary and phytosanitary measures, labeling norms, and product traceability requirements determine market access.

Certification under frameworks aligned with the International Organization for Standardization or compliance with importing-country regulatory bodies often involves multiple audits, documentation protocols, and recurring fees.

For women-led micro and small enterprises, especially those transitioning from informal or semi-formal operations, this creates layered constraints:

- Limited access to technical advisory services
- High upfront audit and inspection costs
- Documentation burdens disproportionate to scale
- Delays in certification cycles affecting working capital

In sectors such as handicrafts, processed foods, natural cosmetics, and community-based products, rigid standardization models often do not adequately reflect small-batch production realities. Without cluster-based certification support or subsidized compliance programs, standards operate as structural filters rather than developmental escalators.

Logistics Costs and Scale Disadvantage

Export viability depends heavily on logistics efficiency. The World Bank Logistics Performance Index underscores how customs efficiency, infrastructure quality, and shipment reliability directly influence trade competitiveness.
Women-led enterprises typically operate at smaller shipment volumes, limiting their bargaining power in freight negotiations. As a result:

- Per-unit transportation costs are higher
- Access to consolidated warehousing is restricted
- Insurance and export documentation costs weigh more heavily on margins
- Delays in port clearance strain liquidity cycles

For enterprises located in rural production clusters or geographically peripheral regions, the asymmetry is amplified. Packaging compliance, labeling standards, and export-grade quality control add further cost layers. In highly competitive global markets, these incremental costs erode price competitiveness and restrict scaling potential.

Digital freight platforms and third-party logistics aggregators are emerging solutions, but uptake requires digital capability, predictable cash flow, and institutional support—conditions not uniformly available.

Digital Marketplace Integration: Access with Conditionality

Cross-border e-commerce has opened new entry points. Platforms such as Amazon and Alibaba Group enable small enterprises to reach global consumers without traditional intermediaries. For women-led ventures, this reduces dependence on export agents and wholesale buyers.

However, digital integration introduces its own structural conditions:

- Platform commission structures and advertising costs
- Algorithm-driven visibility systems
- Compliance with cross-border taxation and consumer protection rules
- Data governance and payment settlement requirements

Exporting digitally requires capacity in digital marketing, analytics, product positioning, and inventory synchronization. Enterprises that lack these capabilities often remain nominal participants with limited scalability. Digital trade lowers entry thresholds, but it does not eliminate competitive asymmetries.

The Strategic Role of Trade Facilitation Agencies

Institutional mediation remains central to enabling equitable export participation. Trade facilitation bodies, export promotion councils, and agencies working in coordination with the International Trade Centre have introduced gender-responsive export readiness programs, certification subsidies, and cluster-based trade models.

- Effective interventions typically combine:
- Export readiness diagnostics
- Subsidized or pooled certification services
- Market intelligence dissemination
- Digital commerce training
- Export credit guarantees and risk mitigation instruments

Where such programs are systematically integrated into national SME strategies, women-led enterprises demonstrate measurable improvements in export entry and diversification. Where policy remains fragmented, outcomes are limited to pilot-scale success stories without structural transformation.

Recalibrating Trade Architecture

The underrepresentation of women-led enterprises in export markets is not a capability deficit. It is largely a systems design issue. Trade regimes, certification frameworks, and logistics infrastructures were historically calibrated around larger firms with established compliance capacities.

A forward-oriented SME policy approach would prioritize:

- Proportional compliance pathways for micro-exporters
- Shared testing and certification infrastructure at cluster levels
- Integrated digital trade facilitation platforms linking customs, standards, and payments
- Gender-responsive trade finance instruments
- Collective export consortia to enhance scale efficiencies

Export participation strengthens enterprise resilience, diversifies revenue streams, and integrates domestic producers into global value chains. For women-led enterprises, sustained participation requires institutional alignment rather than episodic support.

The evolving trade landscape presents opportunity. The decisive factor will be whether policy frameworks, logistics systems, and digital platforms evolve to accommodate diverse enterprise structures while preserving competitiveness and standards integrity.

For small enterprises led by women, global markets are no longer distant. The remaining challenge lies in dismantling structural frictions that continue to shape access.

Mulund is redefining urban living through stronger connectivity, larger flexible homes, and lifestyle-driven residential design. New-age buyers are steering demand toward spacious layouts, community-oriented amenities, and long-term value.

How Mulund's Real Estate Is Adapting to New-Age Buyers

Chintan Sheth

Mulund has long been recognised as one of Mumbai's most liveable and environmentally conscious suburbs. Over the last decade, however, it has undergone a quiet transformation. More than just a residential pocket on the Central line, Mulund has become a micro-market that reflects how the next generation of homebuyers is reshaping expectations—and how developers must evolve accordingly. Young families, first-time buyers, and next-gen professionals now form a significant share of demand, and they come with clearer, more sophisticated priorities.

A New Kind of Buyer Has Emerged

The contemporary homebuyer in Mulund evaluates a property far beyond its carpet area or amenity checklist. Purchasing decisions are driven by functionality, long-term value, and lifestyle alignment.

Young families prioritise open, safe, and child-friendly environments. Professionals increasingly expect homes that enable hybrid work, offer flexibility in room usage, and support productivity without compromising comfort. First-time buy-

First published in the Web Edition of Global SME News. <https://globalsmenews.com/how-mulunds-real-estate-is-adapting-to-new-age-buyers/

ers, meanwhile, have become more discerning. They look past glossy marketing and emphasise timely delivery, transparent documentation, and credible project execution.

In short, the home is no longer perceived as a static asset. It is expected to integrate seamlessly into the rhythms of everyday life—supporting family needs, professional transitions, and lifestyle upgrades.

Why Mulund Stands Out

Mulund's strongest advantage today is its rapidly evolving connectivity. Strategically positioned at the junction of Mumbai's Eastern and Western corridors, it offers easy access to Thane, Navi Mumbai, Powai, and business districts such as BKC.

Upcoming infrastructure upgrades continue to redefine the suburb's prospects. Metro Lines 4 and 5, the Goregaon–Mulund Link Road, and ongoing enhancements to the Eastern Express Highway are poised to cut travel time significantly and open new mobility routes. For professionals balancing workplace demands and for families managing schools, commutes, and leisure, this connectivity offers meaningful value.

Equally important is Mulund's unique relationship with space. In a city where compact one-bedroom apartments have long shaped residential norms, Mulund offers an alternative. Demand for spacious two-bedroom homes has remained robust, while interest in three- and four-bedroom apartments has risen sharply. This reflects a wider shift: families increasingly seek flexibility for home offices, study areas, playrooms, or multi-generational living arrangements. Developers, including us, are responding with larger layouts, adaptable configurations, and designs that reflect modern aspirations.

Lessons for Developers

Mulund offers three critical lessons for the real estate industry:

- Space is a necessity, not a luxury. Buyers expect homes that support evolving family structures and hybrid work lifestyles.
- Connectivity drives confidence. Infrastructure progress reassures buyers that their investment will remain future-ready.
- Lifestyle features are now baseline expectations. Green spaces, wellness amenities, community facilities, and sustainable designs are no longer differentiators—they are essentials.

Today's buyers are informed, digitally savvy, and meticulous. They compare prices, evaluate reputations, and conduct extensive research before making decisions. Developers must therefore prioritise transparency, quality, and value-oriented design.

A Model for the Future

As Mumbai continues to expand, Mulund stands out as a micro-market with a clear blueprint for the future. Buyers invest when homes reflect contemporary aspirations, infrastructure delivers on its promises, and developers look beyond square footage to prioritise liveability and long-term value.

For families, professionals, and first-time buyers, Mulund represents a lifestyle choice grounded in convenience, community, and comfort. For developers, it demonstrates that the future of real estate lies in creating homes people genuinely want to live in—not just spaces to inhabit, but environments that support ambitions, enhance wellbeing, and evolve with time.

As climate shocks intensify and sustainability regulations tighten, small enterprises face rising adaptation costs with limited access to targeted finance. Climate adaptation finance remains concentrated in large infrastructure, leaving MSMEs to absorb flood risks, energy volatility, and compliance pressures largely on their own. Redirecting blended finance, green credit lines, and procurement reforms toward enterprise-level resilience is essential for safeguarding competitiveness, employment, and local economic stability.

Climate Adaptation Finance and the SME Imperative

Svetlana M

Small and medium enterprises operate at the frontline of climate volatility, yet remain at the margins of climate finance architecture. Across emerging and industrial economies alike, enterprises face recurring flood disruptions, heat-induced productivity losses, water scarcity, and volatile energy costs. These are not abstract environmental concerns; they directly affect working capital cycles, asset utilization rates, and long-term business viability. Despite this exposure, adaptation finance continues to be disproportionately directed toward large infrastructure and mitigation-focused projects rather than enterprise-level resilience.

The scale of exposure is economically significant. The International Energy Agency estimates that small and medium-sized enterprises account for more than 13 percent of global final energy demand. In manufacturing-intensive clusters, that share is often considerably higher. Energy efficiency improvements in MSMEs therefore represent not only environmental gains but cost reductions with direct competitiveness effects. However, the upfront investment requirements for efficient machinery, cooling systems, insulation, rooftop solar installations, and digital energy management systems remain a persistent barrier for smaller firms with constrained balance sheets.

Multilateral development banks have expanded climate finance commitments in recent years, with institutions such as the World Bank and the Asian Development Bank reporting record climate-related allocations. Yet mitigation projects—renewable energy parks, grid upgrades, and large transport systems—continue to dominate. Adaptation, especially at the enterprise level, receives a smaller share of total commitments. Where adaptation finance is available, it is frequently structured through sovereign infrastructure channels or large intermediated funds without explicit MSME targeting.

This allocation pattern creates a structural gap. Small enterprises experience the first-order impacts of climate variability but rarely access concessional capital or risk-sharing instruments designed to cushion those impacts. Flood-prone industrial estates require drainage and insurance reform, but individual units also need financing for asset protection, process redesign, and contingency planning. Heat-stressed workshops require cooling retrofits and shift adjustments, yet few targeted credit lines exist to support such adaptation.

Encouragingly, new instruments are emerging. Green credit lines routed through domestic banks, partial credit guarantees, and blended finance facilities are being piloted in multiple regions. In India, initiatives under the Ministry of Micro, Small and Medium Enterprises have begun linking interest subventions and energy audits to MSME technology upgrades. These approaches attempt to lower capital costs while improving project bankability through standardized technical assessments. However, uptake remains uneven. Commercial lenders often lack sector-specific appraisal capacity, and many enterprises struggle with documentation requirements necessary to qualify for concessional windows.

Regulatory shifts in advanced markets are adding a new layer of pressure. Sustainability disclosure frameworks advanced by the European Commission are reshaping supply chain expectations. While reporting obligations primarily apply to larger corporations, compliance cascades downwards. SMEs integrated into export value chains are increasingly required to disclose carbon footprints, energy usage data, and environmental risk exposure. For small suppliers, especially in textiles, agro-processing, light engineering, and artisanal sectors, these requirements represent new administrative and technical costs. Without structured support for measurement and reporting, market access risks may intensify.

Energy transition costs further complicate the landscape. Retrofitting production systems for efficiency often yields attractive medium-term payback periods, but initial capital expenditures deter adoption. Traditional credit appraisal models continue to prioritize collateral over projected cash-flow gains from energy savings. Innovative mechanisms—such as pay-as-you-save models, on-bill financing, and revenue-linked repayments—remain limited in scale and geography. Where they exist, they demonstrate that appropriately structured financial instruments can align repayment schedules with realized savings, reducing perceived risk for both lender and borrower.

Green public procurement represents a parallel opportunity. As governments in Europe and Asia integrate life-cycle emissions criteria into tendering frameworks, demand for low-carbon products and services is expanding. If procurement lots are appropriately sized and accompanied by supplier development programs, SMEs can leverage these standards to upgrade technology and secure predictable markets. However, complex qualification criteria and minimum turnover thresholds often exclude smaller firms. Without deliberate SME-sensitive design, green procurement risks reinforcing concentration rather than broadening participation.

The policy implications are clear. Climate adaptation finance must move beyond macro-level commitments and translate into instruments compatible with MSME operational realities. This requires smaller ticket sizes, simplified compliance templates, mandatory technical assistance components, and aggregation mechanisms that bundle multiple enterprise projects into investable portfolios. Development banks can expand guarantee facilities that reduce first-loss risk for domestic lenders. National MSME agencies can integrate climate resilience explicitly into cluster development programs. Commercial banks can adjust underwriting models to recognize efficiency-linked cash-flow improvements rather than relying exclusively on asset-backed security.

The macroeconomic stakes are substantial. SMEs generate employment intensity, regional supply diversification, and entrepreneurial dynamism. When climate shocks destabilize small enterprises, the resulting disruptions reverberate through local labor markets and national production networks. Adaptation finance structured for MSMEs is therefore not simply an environmental intervention; it is an economic stabilization measure.

As climate volatility becomes structurally embedded in global economic systems, resilience at the enterprise level will determine broader competitiveness trajectories. Redirecting adaptation finance toward MSMEs—through targeted credit lines, blended instruments, compliance support, and procurement reform—is not a peripheral adjustment. It is central to safeguarding productive capacity in an era of accelerating climate risk.

SCALING SMES
Why Governance Matters as Much as Growth

Santanu Sengupta*

Most SMEs don't fail because they lack ambition, innovation, or market opportunity. They fail because governance does not evolve at the same pace as growth.

Having worked closely with boards and advised founder-led enterprises across stages and geographies, I have seen this pattern repeatedly. Entrepreneurs build strong products and gain early traction, but as complexity increases—new markets, new capital, new stakeholders—the absence of governance discipline begins to show. What once felt like agility starts to resemble fragility. Growth continues, but resilience does not.

**Santanu Sengupta is an accomplished senior Global Banking executive, with three decades of leadership experience shaping business growth, governance, risk management, strategy and transformation at leading international banks. As former Managing Director & APAC South Head at Wells Fargo Bank, Singapore, he led diverse businesses and cross-border teams across 15 countries.*

He currently serves as Advisor to Boards & Startups in technology-enabled businesses, bringing contemporary expertise in AI governance, Cyber resilience, ESG stewardship and Digital oversight, to his rich and diversified experience across Finance, Banking, Capital Markets, Risk Management, Global Payments & Trade and Talent& Culture Stewardship.
Santanu is widely recognized for his thought leadership on Responsible Innovation, AI Governance, ESG & Sustainability, Risk Management and Purpose -driven Leadership.

First published in the Web Edition of Global SME News <www.globalsmenews.com>

Governance, in this context, is not about control or compliance. It is about building the institutional muscle required to scale sustainably. And this is where board-level mentoring can be a decisive inflection point for SMEs.

The hidden gap in scaling enterprises

SMEs operate in an environment defined by speed. Decisions are frequent, roles overlap, and priorities shift rapidly. This flexibility is essential in the early phases of growth. However, as organisations scale, informal decision-making, founder-centric authority, and lightweight controls begin to create structural risk.

Boards, by design, bring a different lens. They exist to provide oversight, long-term perspective, and disciplined challenge. When introduced too late, boards are often perceived as bureaucratic overlays and mechanisms that slow down execution. But when board thinking is embedded early, through mentoring rather than enforcement, it creates clarity rather than constraint.

The most resilient SMEs are those that learn to integrate governance into their operating rhythm without sacrificing entrepreneurial energy.

What board-level mentoring brings to scaling SMEs

Risk awareness without risk aversion

Experienced directors do not dilute ambition; they sharpen it. Through board-level mentoring, founders learn to recognise risks that are often invisible during rapid growth eg. regulatory exposure, financial control gaps, data and cyber vulnerabilities, reputational dependencies.

Addressing these early does not slow momentum. It reduces disruption. SMEs that anticipate risk rather than react to crises retain strategic optionality as they scale.

Decision frameworks that grow with the organisation

As SMEs expand, the volume and complexity of decisions increase dramatically. What works with a small leadership team becomes inconsistent across larger, distributed teams.

Board mentors introduce scalable decision frameworks including clarity on authority, escalation, and accountability. These frameworks do not replace founder judgment; they institutionalise it. Over time, they enable faster, better-aligned decisions across the organisation.

Credibility with capital providers and regulators

Capital today is increasingly selective. Investors and lenders differentiate not just on growth metrics, but on governance quality. Strong governance signals maturity, predictability, and stewardship.

SMEs with board-level discipline navigate funding discussions, regulatory engagement, and stakeholder scrutiny with greater confidence. They answer difficult questions proactively, not defensively. In many cases, governance becomes a tangible differentiator in accessing better capital on better terms.

Succession and continuity beyond the founder

Many SMEs are built around the founder's vision, energy, and relationships. While this concentration of leadership can accelerate early growth, it becomes a vulnerability as scale increases.

Board-level mentoring encourages founders to build leadership depth, clarify roles, and plan for continuity. Succession is not a sign of exit intent; it is a sign of institutional maturity. Enterprises that address this early are better equipped to navigate transitions without value erosion.

Financial discipline as a strategic capability

Growth can obscure weak financial discipline, until it no longer can. Cash flow governance, reporting rigor, compliance discipline, and capital allocation frameworks are often introduced reactively, under pressure.

Board mentors help embed these disciplines early, transforming finance from a reporting function into a strategic capability. The result is not conservatism, but sustainability.

Misconceptions that hold SMEs back

From the SME perspective, boards are often viewed as necessary only at scale, or as mechanisms imposed by investors. Governance is seen as something to be "added later."

From the board perspective, SMEs can appear informal, chaotic, or under-structured, leading some directors to default to rigid governance models that are ill-suited to entrepreneurial environments.

Both perspectives miss the opportunity.
Smart founders see governance as an accelerator, not a brake.
Smart directors see SMEs as environments where governance must be adaptive, proportionate, and context-aware.

The real bridge: board-level mentoring
The most effective bridge between entrepreneurial speed and institutional discipline is not compliance, it is mentoring.

Board-level mentoring respects the pace at which SMEs operate while gradually embedding the structures required for scale. It focuses on asking better questions, not prescribing rigid answers. It helps founders transition from operators to stewards, without losing their entrepreneurial edge.

This approach transforms governance from an obligation into an asset.
A maturing SME ecosystem

Across markets, SMEs are entering a more demanding phase of growth. Stakeholders including investors, regulators, partners, and customers expect greater transparency, accountability, and resilience.

The next generation of successful SMEs will not be defined by innovation alone. They will be defined by their ability to institutionalise good judgment.

Growth creates opportunity.
Governance determines longevity.
The most enduring enterprises are those that recognise this early, before scale exposes what governance failed to prepare.

Old password leaks do not disappear with time; they circulate, mutate, and quietly power today's fraud economy. What appears as a "new breach" is often the resurfacing of historic data, made dangerous by predictable user behavior. Understanding this hidden afterlife is critical to reducing long-term digital risk.

Data Breaches Have Memory

*How Old Passwords Continue to Threaten Users**

*Rakesh Raghuvanshi***

It is often said that the internet never forgets. And while this line is mostly used in the context of someone's old tweets resurfacing, there is a far more sinister meaning that we don't talk about enough.

This week, reports of a "Gmail password breach" flooded social media, sparking panic and confusion. Headlines screamed that millions of Gmail accounts had been compromised. But soon, Google issued a clarification saying that its systems were not hacked. The leaked passwords, the tech giant added, came from older data dumps, that is, massive archives of stolen credentials compiled from years of unrelated breaches, phishing kits, and malware infections.

In other words, this was not a new breach at all. It was a compilation of many older ones stitched together.

As usual, some believe that there was a breach and others believes the rebuttal. Researchers are still trying to ascertain exactly whose version is correct.

Whatever the case, the incident shows how the life cycle of a data breach nev-

***Mr. Rakesh Raghuvanshi is the Founder and CEO of Sekel Tech*

**First published in the Web Edition of Global SME News <www.globalsmenews.com>*

er truly ends. Once a password is exposed, it becomes part of the digital black market's permanent memory. Hackers package and repackage it, add it to new "combo lists," and circulate it on underground forums or messaging channels where credentials are bought, sold, or shared freely.

That is why I often call breaches immortal. The stolen data keeps coming back in new forms, long after the original hack fades from memory.

A password leaked from a small e-commerce site in 2017, for instance, might still be sitting in a breach compilation today, combined with data from a different platform. Cybercriminals then feed these lists into automated software programs that enter different username-password pairs across multiple websites. This is known as "credential stuffing" and these tools can test millions of combinations per minute.

In simpler words, this means that if you have used the save password anywhere, be it your Gmail, your Instagram, or your online banking, it's only a matter of time before one of those attempts succeeds.

Old breach data is valuable because it's cheap, abundant, and useful. It is traded everywhere, from private dark web forums to open Telegram groups and file-sharing sites. Sellers even advertise "fresh compilations" of previously leaked data, sometimes mixing it with a few new elements to make it appear recent.

This recycling economy is what fuels the current wave of impersonation scams and investment frauds. Attackers don't need your live password to trick your contacts. They only need your old one to find out where you've registered, what services you use, or which accounts you might have abandoned. Armed with that information, scammers can build convincing phishing messages that look personal. "We noticed a suspicious login on your Flipkart account," is a classic example.

The problem isn't that hackers are innovative. The problem is that humans are predictable. Many users still reuse the same password across multiple accounts, sometimes for convenience, sometimes because they underestimate the risk. When a decade-old password is still active anywhere, it acts as a skeleton key across your digital life.

Even password resets don't always help. If your recovery email or phone number hasn't changed in years, a scammer can use information from an old breach to trigger password-reset requests, hijack secondary accounts, and lock you out before you notice.

Protecting yourself from old data breaches isn't about learning cybersecurity jargon. It's about changing habits that hackers rely on. Some quick daily habits can be to never reuse passwords, turn on two-factor authentication (an OTP or verification link as an extra layer of protection), not ignore breach notifications and be wary of messages or emails that reference old accounts.

The Gmail incident may have been a false alarm, but it carried a real lesson. Data breaches are not isolated incidents; they are thriving ecosystems on the dark web that only grow over time. Every leak adds to a vast, living archive of personal information that keeps expanding and resurfacing.

On the other hand, however, a breach may be immortal, but its impact on you doesn't have to be.

The global DTDB market was valued at approximately USD 1.2 billion in 2024 and is projected to reach USD 3.8 billion by 2033, growing at a compound annual growth rate (CAGR) of 13.7 percent during the 2025–2033 period.

Digital Terrain Database Market Set to Reach USD 3.8 Billion by 2033

Chris Peterson

In an era where intelligence is increasingly spatial, Digital Terrain Databases (DTDBs) are emerging as a critical backbone of modern digital infrastructure. Once confined to specialised military and mapping applications, terrain intelligence is now central to urban planning, climate resilience, autonomous systems, and high-precision engineering. Reflecting this shift, the global Digital Terrain Database market is entering a phase of sustained expansion.

According to Research Intelo, the global DTDB market was valued at approximately USD 1.2 billion in 2024 and is projected to reach USD 3.8 billion by 2033, growing at a compound annual growth rate (CAGR) of 13.7 percent during the 2025–2033 period. The growth underscores a broader transformation in how physical landscapes are digitised, analysed, and integrated into decision-making systems.

First published in the Web Edition of Global SME News <www.globalsmenews.com>

From Mapping to Terrain Intelligence

Digital Terrain Databases go far beyond conventional digital maps. They are structured, multi-layered repositories of elevation models, landform geometry, surface textures, hydrology, and geospatial attributes designed for analytical precision. Unlike visual navigation tools, DTDBs are engineered for simulation, modelling, and predictive analysis.

This makes them indispensable for applications where centimetre-level accuracy can determine operational success—ranging from defence mission planning to flood forecasting and autonomous navigation. Increasingly, terrain data is being treated not as a static reference layer, but as a dynamic intelligence asset.

Key Drivers of Market Growth

The accelerating adoption of DTDBs is being driven by a convergence of strategic, environmental, and technological factors.

Defence modernisation remains one of the strongest demand drivers. Armed forces rely on high-resolution terrain data for route planning, surveillance, targeting, and battlefield simulation, enabling forces to anticipate terrain constraints before deployment.

Climate change and disaster risk management are also pushing demand. Accurate terrain data plays a crucial role in flood modelling, landslide prediction, coastal vulnerability assessment, and environmental monitoring, supporting early-warning systems and resilience planning.

Urbanisation and infrastructure development further fuel market growth. Smart city initiatives and large infrastructure projects require precise elevation and surface modelling for drainage design, zoning, transport corridors, and construction safety.

Additionally, the rapid rise of autonomous systems—from drones to self-driving vehicles—has made terrain intelligence essential. Autonomous platforms depend on accurate geospatial and elevation data to navigate complex and unpredictable environments safely.

Technology Shaping the DTDB Ecosystem

Advances in geospatial technologies are redefining the capabilities of digital terrain databases. High-resolution LiDAR and hyperspectral imaging enable detailed terrain reconstruction, while artificial intelligence and machine learning automate terrain classification and pattern detection across vast datasets.

Cloud-native platforms are improving scalability and global accessibility, allowing terrain data to be processed and updated continuously. At the same time, edge computing is enabling real-time terrain analysis for time-critical applications such as autonomous navigation and defence operations. The adoption of 3D and 4D terrain modelling is also expanding, allowing landscapes to be analysed not only in space but across time.

Expanding Application Areas

DTDB adoption is broadening across multiple industries. In construction and civil engineering, terrain data supports planning for highways, rail networks, tunnels, and airports. In oil, gas, and mining, it improves exploration efficiency, access planning, and risk management. Agriculture and forestry increasingly use terrain analytics for precision irrigation, soil optimisation, and land-use planning. Aerospace and aviation applications include terrain-aware flight planning and landing safety assessments.

Challenges and Market Outlook

Despite strong growth prospects, the market faces challenges, including integrating heterogeneous datasets, maintaining up-to-date terrain models in rapidly changing environments, ensuring cybersecurity for sensitive applications, and balancing ultra-high resolution with storage and processing costs.

However, these challenges are driving further innovation rather than slowing adoption. Investment is increasingly focused on automated terrain updates, real-time sensing, and advanced data fusion.

Looking ahead, the Digital Terrain Database market is expected to evolve from descriptive mapping toward predictive terrain intelligence. Future systems are likely to integrate real-time environmental monitoring, digital twins of land surfaces, and satellite-linked automated updates, enabling organisations not just to understand terrain—but to anticipate how it will change.

As digital systems become more deeply embedded in physical space, terrain intelligence is set to become a silent yet indispensable pillar of the global digital economy.

FROM SURVIVAL TO STRATEGY

How MSMEs Are Redefining Growth in a Fragmented Global Economy

Rupam Tandon*

For much of the past decade, the MSME narrative has revolved around survival — navigating pandemics, supply-chain shocks, inflation, and capital constraints. Today, that narrative is decisively changing. Across regions, MSMEs and startups are no longer just adapting to disruption; they are strategically reshaping how growth is defined and delivered in a fractured global economy.

The current environment is marked by geopolitical realignment, higher interest rates, shifting trade corridors, and rapid technological acceleration. In this context, traditional growth models built on scale, leverage, and cost arbitrage are losing relevance. What is emerging instead is a new MSME playbook grounded in resilience, agility, and trust.

Three structural shifts stand out.

First, resilience has overtaken expansion as a strategic priority. MSMEs are strengthening balance sheets, diversifying suppliers, regionalising supply chains, and taking a more disciplined approach to capital deployment. Growth is being pursued with risk awareness, not blind optimism. This shift is particularly visible among export-oriented SMEs and venture-backed startups recalibrating their paths to profitability.

Second, digital capability is no longer optional or experimental. Cloud platforms, data analytics, AI-enabled tools, and digital payments have become core operating infrastructure. For MSMEs, technology is not just improving efficiency; it is enabling compliance, transparency, customer access, and cross-border participation. Digital maturity increasingly determines whether an enterprise can integrate into global value chains.

Third, trust has become a decisive economic asset. Access to capital, partnerships, and markets is now influenced by governance quality, ethical conduct, and ESG credibility. MSMEs are discovering that sustainability reporting, sound governance practices, and workforce responsibility are not burdens imposed by regulators or large enterprises — they are enablers of long-term relevance and competitiveness.

Public policy plays a defining role in this transition. Governments that simplify regulation, improve credit access, invest in digital public infrastructure, and create predictable policy environments are accelerating MSME formalisation and growth. Conversely, fragmented compliance regimes, policy uncertainty, and high transaction costs continue to suppress enterprise potential, particularly in emerging markets.Across boardrooms, policy discussions, and enterprise engagements, this shift from survival to strategy is already underway.

The next decade of global growth will not be driven solely by large corporations or capital-heavy models. It will be shaped by MSMEs that can align strategy with resilience, technology with trust, and ambition with governance. In a world where uncertainty is the norm, adaptability has become the most valuable form of scale.

For MSMEs and startups, the question is no longer how to survive disruption — but how to lead through it.

** Rupam Tandon is a seasoned financial services leader, global strategist, and board advisor with over three decades of experience across investment banking, strategic advisory, and corporate governance. Having held senior roles with leading international institutions, she brings deep expertise in banking, compliance, risk management, and organizational transformation across India, the United Kingdom, the United Arab Emirates, and North Africa. A Certified Independent Director and respected governance advocate, she advises boards and scaling enterprises on embedding risk discipline and ethical leadership into growth strategies.*

A recognised thought leader in startup governance, Rupam contributed a specialist chapter to Enterprising Futures: Global SME Insights 2025, highlighting governance as a strategic lever for resilience and investor confidence. She actively mentors women leaders, guides founders on governance readiness, and champions responsible leadership as the foundation of long-term enterprise value creation.

As the global MSME finance gap persists at multi-trillion-dollar levels, fintech-driven embedded lending, revenue-based models, and supply-chain finance are reshaping how small enterprises access working capital—offering adaptive solutions that challenge traditional collateral-driven banking frameworks.

Alternative Finance Beyond Banks

Fintech, Revenue-Based Lending and Supply-Chain Finance in a Constrained Credit Environment

Svetlana M

Micro and small enterprises operate within complex economic environments where access to finance continues to function as a structural bottleneck rather than a temporary market imperfection. The financing challenge is not marginal. According to assessments by the World Bank and the International Finance Corporation, the global MSME finance gap in emerging markets is estimated at approximately US$5.7 trillion for formal enterprises alone, rising substantially when informal firms are considered.

This gap is not simply a reflection of risk aversion. It is rooted in institutional design. Traditional banking frameworks prioritize collateral, audited balance sheets, and standardized financial documentation. Many small enterprises—particularly those in services, digital trade, local manufacturing, handicrafts, and distributed supply systems—operate with thin asset bases and irregular cash-flow documentation. Their exclusion is therefore systemic, not incidental.

In this context, alternative finance models have moved from experimental niches to increasingly relevant instruments within the SME ecosystem. Fintech-enabled embedded finance, revenue-based lending (RBL), and supply-chain finance (SCF) are not substitutes for banking; they are adaptive responses to its structural limitations.

Embedded finance integrates credit within digital ecosystems where enterprises already transact—marketplaces, payment gateways, accounting platforms, and enterprise software systems. Underwriting relies on transactional data rather than physical collateral. Sales velocity, invoice turnover, receivables patterns, and digital payment histories become primary credit indicators. This reduces information asymmetry and shortens decision cycles. For working capital–intensive SMEs, particularly in retail distribution and platform-based commerce, such models align financing with real-time business activity.

However, the rapid growth of embedded lending raises regulatory and governance questions. Licensing categories often lag behind innovation. Disclosure standards vary across jurisdictions. Data ownership and portability remain unevenly defined. In the absence of proportionate oversight, platform concentration risks may intensify, with SMEs becoming dependent on a limited number of dominant digital intermediaries.

Revenue-based lending represents another structural shift. Instead of fixed monthly repayments, enterprises repay a predetermined share of revenue until a capped return multiple is reached. This model is particularly suited to enterprises with recurring sales patterns or aggregator-linked turnover streams. By linking repayment to actual revenue flows, RBL reduces stress during seasonal downturns and aligns financing with cash-flow realities rather than rigid amortization schedules.

Yet transparency remains critical. Many RBL structures communicate pricing through repayment multiples without translating cost into comparable annualized metrics. From a market integrity perspective, standardized disclosure norms would enhance borrower awareness and enable rational comparison across financial products.

Supply-chain finance, meanwhile, leverages the credit strength of anchor corporates to unlock liquidity for smaller suppliers. Through reverse factoring mechanisms, suppliers receive early payment on approved invoices, while financiers recover funds from the larger buyer at maturity. The International Finance Corporation has consistently emphasized supply-chain finance as a scalable instrument to address working capital constraints within structured value chains. Where digital invoicing systems and enforceable receivables frameworks are in place, SCF can significantly lower financing costs for smaller firms.

However, SCF is inherently chain-dependent. Enterprises operating outside organized supply networks remain excluded. Moreover, concentrated buyer structures may introduce systemic exposure if liquidity access becomes anchored to a small number of corporates. Legal infrastructure—factoring laws, collateral registries, digital enforceability of receivables—remains foundational to scaling SCF sustainably.

A parallel transformation is visible in credit assessment methodologies. Increasingly, lenders incorporate digital footprints into underwriting models. POS data, e-commerce transaction histories, utility payment behavior, tax filing records, and supply-chain invoice flows contribute to alternative credit scoring frameworks. The World Bank and the International Finance Corporation underscore the role of digital financial infrastructure in narrowing the MSME credit gap.

While digital scoring expands inclusion, it introduces governance concerns. Algorithmic bias, opaque decision logic, and data privacy vulnerabilities can undermine trust. Effective regulatory design must therefore balance innovation with borrower protection—ensuring explainability, consent-based data use, and appeal mechanisms for credit decisions.

The evolution of alternative finance signals a broader transition in SME credit architecture. Financial intermediation is becoming data-driven, platform-integrated, and value-chain anchored. Yet scale will depend on institutional coherence. Policymakers must enable proportionate licensing frameworks, transparent pricing standards, digital public infrastructure, and systemic risk monitoring. Development finance institutions can catalyze early-stage market development through risk-sharing mechanisms and technical assistance.

The global MSME finance gap remains large. But the contours of response are clearer than before. Where innovation is supported by robust governance and digital infrastructure, alternative finance can move beyond episodic experimentation and become a durable pillar in the ecosystem of small enterprise development.

Amul and IFFCO have secured the top two positions in the International Cooperative Alliance's World Cooperative Monitor 2025 rankings, underscoring the global impact of India's cooperative ecosystem. Their rise reflects the strength of collective enterprise models that integrate millions of small producers into organised value chains while maintaining local ownership and community-driven governance. This global recognition highlights the continued relevance of cooperatives in building inclusive, resilient, and scalable enterprise systems.

Amul and IFFCO Top Global Rankings: A New Benchmark for Inclusive Enterprise Models

The International Cooperative Alliance's World Cooperative Monitor 2025 has placed two Indian institutions—Amul (GCMMF) and IFFCO—at the very top of its global cooperative rankings. Amul secured the number one position while IFFCO followed closely at number two, marking a significant milestone for Asia's cooperative sector and reaffirming the global competitiveness of India's community-owned enterprise models. The ranking uses a methodology based on turnover relative to GDP per capita, a metric designed to capture the relative economic weight and societal impact of cooperative enterprises rather than their absolute revenue scale.

This recognition arrives at a moment when small producers, micro-enterprises, and rural communities across developing regions continue to face structural constraints—particularly in finance, market access, and bargaining power. In such

**First published in the Web Edition of Global SME News <www.globalsmenews.com>*

contexts, cooperatives provide a robust institutional alternative, delivering economies of scale, collective risk-sharing, and democratic governance structures that often outperform fragmented small-holder approaches.

A Model Rooted in Local Participation

Amul's ascent to the top is grounded in a highly decentralised network of 18,600 village-level dairy cooperatives, representing nearly 3.6 million milk producers. The cooperative structure allows dispersed producers to aggregate output, negotiate better market prices, and access processing and distribution systems that would otherwise be unavailable to micro dairy farmers operating individually. Its ability to integrate millions of small producers into organised value chains distinguishes Amul from many global competitors.

Similarly, IFFCO—supported by 35,000 member cooperatives and reaching nearly 50 million farmers—demonstrates the potential of cooperative institutions to serve agricultural input markets at industrial scale. By pooling demand from millions of farmers, IFFCO ensures stable access to fertilisers, introduces technology interventions efficiently, and maintains price stability in a sector often vulnerable to supply chain shocks.

Collective enterprise models enable scale while preserving local ownership.

Amul and IFFCO's performance underscores a broader theme relevant to the SME ecosystem: collective enterprise structures can deliver scale without compromising local ownership. This is particularly important in contexts where micro and small enterprises struggle with:

- lack of formal collateral
- inconsistent cash flows
- limited negotiating capacity
- information asymmetry in pricing and procurement markets

Cooperatives offer a mechanism through which small producers can participate in markets with enhanced bargaining power and improved access to finance and technology. Their success also provides a template for building inclusive business models that strengthen community-based entrepreneurship.

These achievements are also relevant for the future architecture of enterprise development in agricultural and rural sectors. At a time when supply chains face climate-related disruptions and input markets are experiencing volatility, cooperative systems display resilience by virtue of their decentralised networks and member-driven governance.

A Case for Renewed Policy Attention

India's cooperative success story suggests the need for a renewed policy conversation on how cooperative principles can be applied across emerging segments—such as digital services, artisanal enterprises, local food processing, and renewable energy micro-grids. For SME development frameworks, the cooperative model offers advantages that conventional credit-led or purely private-sector models often fail to capture, particularly for informal or grassroots entrepreneurs.

The recognition of Amul and IFFCO by the ICA also reinforces the importance of public systems that support collective institutions—from capacity building and digital platforms to governance reforms and financial inclusion mechanisms. As governments across Asia, Africa, and Latin America explore new strategies for inclusive enterprise growth, the Indian example demonstrates how cooperatives can integrate small producers into national and global value chains without sacrificing local autonomy.

Amul and IFFCO's top global rankings are more than institutional achievements; they represent the growing maturity of India's cooperative architecture. Their success affirms that community-owned enterprises can operate at world-class efficiency, create sustainable livelihoods, and reshape rural economies at scale. For the broader SME discourse, these cooperatives stand as evidence that inclusive models—rooted in local participation and collective governance—remain essential for resilient and equitable economic development

In the bioeconomy, economic activity is anchored in biological processes, biomaterials, and renewable inputs rather than fossil-fuel-dependent industrial structures.

Bioeconomy, Circular Economy, and Post-Growth Paradigms: Rethinking Economic Expansion

Svetlana M

The growing interest in bioeconomy and circular economy frameworks represents a significant departure from the orthodox logic of linear, growth-centric capitalism. At their core, these emerging paradigms challenge the established assumption that economic progress must be tied to continuous material expansion. Instead, they argue for production systems rooted in ecological regeneration, renewable biological resources, and responsible consumption cycles. This shift has profound implications for how enterprises operate and how policymakers conceptualize development itself.

In the bioeconomy, economic activity is anchored in biological processes, biomaterials, and renewable inputs rather than fossil-fuel-dependent industrial structures. Similarly, circular economy practices seek to minimize waste by designing products for reuse, repair, and recycling, thereby extending value chains and reducing environmental stress. Together, these approaches introduce a resource-conscious production model that counters the depletion-driven dynamics of conventional growth.

**First published in the Web Edition of Global SME News <www.globalsmenews.com>*

Such transitions, however, are neither automatic nor cost-free. They require systemic adjustments in technology deployment, industrial organization, and regulatory practice. Enterprises may need to redesign operations around low-carbon processes, invest in biomass-based inputs, or adopt more complex value-recovery mechanisms. Governments, in turn, face the task of establishing coherent policy incentives—ranging from green standards to pricing mechanisms for waste, materials, and emissions—that support circularity across sectors.

A move towards post-growth paradigms inevitably raises questions about trade-offs. Shifting to regenerative production may slow conventional metrics of output expansion, especially in resource-intensive sectors. Labour structures could change, with some industries becoming more knowledge-intensive while others adopt more localized, labour-rich production cycles based on repair, maintenance, and material recovery. There may also be distributional impacts: communities dependent on extractive sectors may face adjustment pressures, while new opportunities emerge in bio-based manufacturing, green chemistry, or sustainable agriculture.

Yet these trade-offs also open space for rethinking development beyond traditional GDP targets. By prioritizing ecological health, long-term resilience, and resource circularity, bioeconomy and post-growth frameworks challenge policymakers to consider what forms of economic activity genuinely contribute to societal well-being. They invite a shift from quantity-driven expansion to quality-oriented transformation—one where innovation is measured not merely by output volumes but by the capacity to regenerate ecosystems, reduce dependency on finite resources, and build socio-economic systems that remain viable for future generations.

This debate extends far beyond enterprise models. It touches on cultural attitudes toward consumption, institutional path dependencies, and the political economy of transition. Whether bioeconomy and circular economy models can scale effectively will depend on how societies navigate these structural, policy, and cultural shifts. But their emergence signals a critical moment: a recognition that the pursuit of endless growth is increasingly incompatible with planetary limits, and that alternative economic systems rooted in sustainability may offer more resilient pathways for development.

AI Unlocks Cancer's Hidden Biology, Paving the Way for Truly Personalized Therapy

Svetlana M

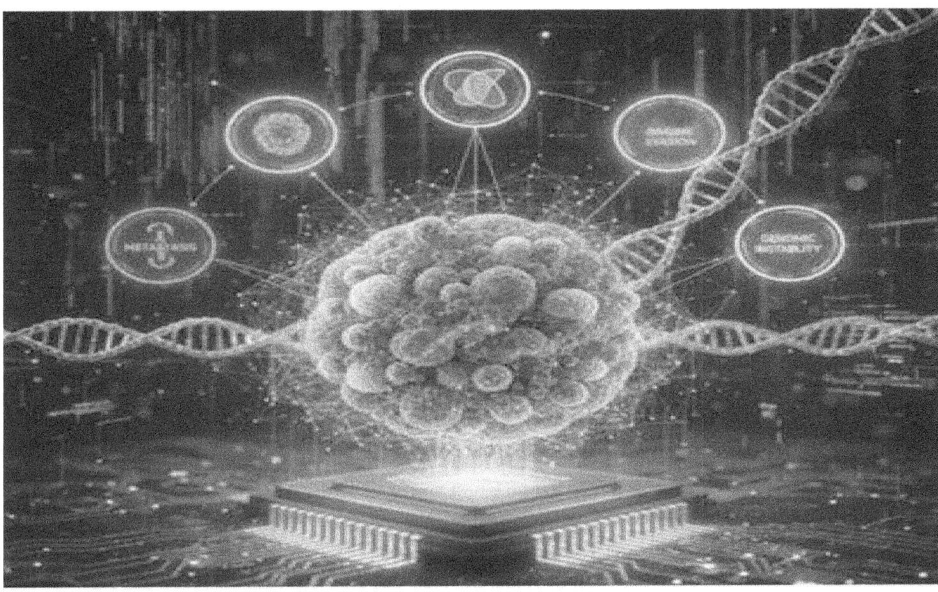

A new artificial intelligence framework developed in India is reshaping how scientists interpret the biology of cancer, opening the door to a more precise and mechanistic approach to treatment. Moving beyond conventional clinical staging, the study reframes cancer as a dynamic system driven by deeply embedded molecular programs—known as the hallmarks of cancer—that determine how tumors grow, spread, and resist therapy.

For decades, oncology has relied on descriptive systems like TNM, which categorize tumors based on size, lymph-node involvement, and metastasis. While useful

**First published in the Web Edition of Global SME News <www.globalsmenews.com>*

for broad classification, these systems fail to capture the molecular heterogeneity that often separates good responders from poor responders—even among patients with the "same" stage. The new framework, OncoMark, developed by scientists at the S N Bose National Centre for Basic Sciences in collaboration with Ashoka University, directly tackles this gap by decoding the molecular "personality" of cancer.

Mapping Cancer's Hidden Programs

Cancer progression is shaped by a set of hallmark processes such as immune evasion, metastasis, genomic instability, angiogenesis, and resistance to cell death. These hallmarks operate at the cellular level long before clinical symptoms emerge. OncoMark uses advanced neural networks to make these invisible processes measurable.

The research team, led by Dr. Shubhasis Haldar and Dr. Debayan Gupta, analyzed 3.1 million single cells from 14 cancer types, creating synthetic pseudo-biopsies that simulate hallmark-driven tumor states. This unprecedented dataset allowed the AI to learn how hallmark activities interact to drive tumor aggression, treatment evasion, or rapid progression.

A central output of the system is its ability to visualize hallmark activation across cancer stages. This provides a new layer of diagnostic insight: two tumors that appear identical in stage may, in fact, possess radically different underlying biology—and require distinct treatment strategies.

Accuracy Across Real-World Patient Samples

OncoMark demonstrated exceptional predictive capability. The framework reported over 99 percent accuracy in internal testing and remained above 96 percent across five independent cohorts. Its robustness was further established through validation on 20,000 patient samples from eight major global datasets, highlighting its potential applicability across population groups and cancer types.

Importantly, the system does not merely classify tumors; it predicts which hallmark programs are active in an individual patient's cancer. This capability can guide clinicians toward drugs that specifically target those biological pathways, creating a pathway for personalized therapy rooted in molecular behavior rather than broad-stage categories.

Pushing Oncology Toward Precision

By offering clinicians a deeper view of tumor biology, OncoMark can help identify cancers that might appear less aggressive under standard staging but exhibit hallmarks associated with rapid progression. This supports earlier intervention and more tailored treatment plans. Conversely, the framework could help avoid overtreatment in cases where hallmark activity suggests indolent disease.

Published in Communications Biology (Nature Publishing Group), the study represents a significant advance in the integration of AI with molecular oncology. As precision medicine continues to evolve, tools such as OncoMark demonstrate how computational modeling can illuminate the biological scripts that drive cancer—and enable therapies that respond to those scripts.

Precast Technology in Construction: Transforming the Homebuying Experience

Jash Panchamia*

Mumbai is a hub for construction activity, and a short drive around is enough for one to experience the sound of concrete mixers, swirling dust, and endless commotion. This is the usual scene at any construction site in Mumbai. But think of a situation that is something far more composed, where there are no ready-mix concrete trucks lining up on-site but instead, there are ready-made building parts arriving quietly and being slotted together with surprising ease. The air around feels a lot cleaner and the ground is clear of waste, with the steady hum of organised work replacing the regular chaos.

As India moves ahead on the path of progress so is the construction industry. You may have read about AI, along with AR and VR being used widely, but what is also making a silent revolution is the use of precast technology. As urbanisation accelerates the demand for affordable, high-quality homes growing, the construction industry is turning a leaf with the use of precast technology. The cleaner and less chaotic construction site that one gets with using precast is also the reason it promises to redefine how homes are built and delivered.

The advantages at site include workers get to breathe better air, neighbours notice less noise, and buyers will notice how the project progresses at a steady,

Mr. Jash Panchamia, Promoter, Suraksha Smart City

First published in the Web Edition of Global SME News <www.globalsmenews.com>

more assured pace. This is the difference precast construction is about. It ensures that factory level precision comes to building sites, it acts against pollution, saves time, and leads through a much calmer, and a more sustainable way to build homes. This is an advantage to the construction industry, especially in our crowded cities, where space and clean air come at a premium.

The other quiet revolution that precast technology has given India's housing sector is the ability to build affordable and high-quality homes. With the demand for this at a peak the construction industry is seeing the value that precast holds. How this technology works is that walls, slabs, staircases, and even entire 3D modules are made in a controlled factory environment. Once cast and ready they are moved to the construction site for assembly. This is a very different approach from conventional labour-intensive methods. The reliance on a heavy on-site work model spread across vast areas is absent. The method here ensures that the bulk of building works take place under stringent quality controls within a regulated atmosphere. This shift is beyond just procedural and fundamentally enhances the whole homebuying experience.

For prospective homeowners, the benefits are tangible. Components made in a factory are stronger and dimensionally accurate. They also consistently remain high in quality, limiting the possibility of defects and the need to undertake costly repairs. Construction timelines come down by a significant margin, as site preparation and factory production can occur simultaneously. This allows residents to get possession of their new homes faster. Safety forms another critical advantage, with controlled factory environments reducing workplace hazards. On-site assembly also demands less labour and involves fewer risks of accidents.

Since sustainability is an increasingly important aspect of modern construction, and precast methods support eco-friendly practices is also becomes a direction for greener building practices. In addition, the precision followed by the assembly process lowers on-site scope of any disruption, providing a more pleasant working environment for communities under development.

Although construction with precast as a technology is fast progressing its adoption. In the context of the Indian market is not moving in equal measure. But this is also changing with ease of obtaining capital investment set to make setting up precast factories a simpler process. Transporting large concrete modules and standardising designs to accommodate diverse local architectural styles are seen as part of logistical hurdles which will ease when the pace of adoption goes up. Similarly, the availability of a skilled labour force for on-site assembly remains in short supply in various parts of India towards which developers are investing in training to fully realise the technology's potential.

As these areas of challenge get addressed through various policy initiatives, the outlook for precast technology in India is upbeat with advancements in 3D casting and use of digital tools like Building Information Modelling (BIM) improving precision and enabling customised designs that accelerate construction. Large-scale developers are betting strongly on setting up precast factories, which is signal toward corporate commitment to innovation, sustainability, and timely delivery. For homebuyers, this is as transformative as it can get. Precast construction methods are a mode of faster project delivery of developments that are structurally robust, resilient, and built to meet modern safety and seismic standards. Even as cost overruns are minimised, timelines get predictable, and the overall living experience is enhanced.

Finally, in a market where traditional construction methods are often slow, labour-intensive, and prone to quality fluctuations, precast technology has set a new benchmark. By combining speed, precision, sustainability, and safety, it has made quality housing more accessible and reliable for millions of Indians. As the industry welcomes mechanisation and modern construction techniques, precast construction has now become a strategic innovation that will reshape India's housing landscape, so that the homes of tomorrow are delivered with greater certainty, efficiency, and care.

LogRhythm | Exabeam has expanded its Saudi presence through a strengthened partnership with MIS and the launch of a Customer Innovation Center in Riyadh, reinforcing enterprise cybersecurity capabilities as the Kingdom accelerates its digital transformation.

LogRhythm | Exabeam Expands Saudi Presence with MIS Partnership and New Customer Innovation Center in Riyadh

Svetlana M

LogRhythm | Exabeam has announced a significant expansion of its Saudi Arabian operations through a strengthened partnership with Al Moammar Information Systems Co. (MIS) and the establishment of a Customer Innovation Center in Riyadh. The developments mark a notable consolidation of the company's presence in a market where cybersecurity capabilities are becoming central to economic transformation and national infrastructure resilience.

MIS, one of the Kingdom's largest publicly listed IT enterprises with annual revenues exceeding SAR 1.2 billion, will jointly deliver LogRhythm SIEM and the Exabeam New-Scale Security Operations Platform to organizations across Saudi Arabia. The collaboration is designed to reinforce enterprise preparedness against advanced cyberthreats, particularly as AI-enabled attacks and organized

**First published in the Web Edition of Global SME News <www.globalsmenews.com>*

cybercrime intensify in frequency and complexity.

LogRhythm | Exabeam reported 21 percent revenue growth in the Kingdom between 2024 and 2025, reflecting the growing demand for integrated, AI-driven threat detection and automated incident response systems. Company executives emphasised that the partnership enables more robust local support, tighter integration with security teams, and faster deployment of next-generation security operations capabilities.

The launch of the Customer Innovation Center in Riyadh signals a deeper commitment to localized knowledge, demonstrating advanced AI applications across IT, OT, and IoT environments. It forms part of a wider set of investments that include the opening of a new office and the appointment of sector-specific leadership roles covering defence, royal institutions, security agencies, public sector entities, and banking and financial industries.

Executives from both organizations stated that the strengthened partnership addresses an urgent market need: as Saudi Arabia's digital interfaces expand, enterprise systems require more adaptive tools to secure mission-critical data and maintain operational continuity. The combined offering from MIS and LogRhythm | Exabeam is positioned to support organizations seeking to modernize their security operations in line with the Kingdom's broader digital transformation priorities.

Through these initiatives, LogRhythm | Exabeam is reinforcing its long-term operational base in Saudi Arabia and scaling its ability to support a rapidly evolving cybersecurity ecosystem.

Distributed Digital Natives: How a New Entrepreneurial Class Is Rewriting Innovation Ecosystems

Chris Peterson

A quiet but decisive shift is shaping the architecture of modern innovation systems. A new cohort—digitally fluent, globally networked, and structurally different from the enterprise models celebrated in earlier phases of industrial development—is beginning to redefine how value is created, exchanged, and scaled. These distributed digital natives operate beyond the traditional markers of business formation. Their ventures emerge from cloud-based infrastructures, rely on algorithmic tools rather than fixed assets, and reach global markets without the sequencing of capital, collateral, or physical expansion that development frameworks once assumed.

First published in the Web Edition of Global SME News <www.globalsmenews.com>

Recent scholarship on digital entrepreneurship underlines this transition. Studies mapping global research trends point to a movement away from firm-level analysis towards a socio-technical understanding of digital value creation. Digital platforms, data flows, and AI-driven production systems increasingly function as factors of production in their own right. Parallel research highlights how these actors behave as nodes within transnational networks rather than participants in bounded domestic ecosystems. This has direct implications for how innovation is understood, how markets are shaped, and how countries configure the environments in which entrepreneurship evolves.

The rise of distributed digital natives can be observed across several patterns. Young creators offering design, content, and analytics services operate on global marketplaces through micro-contracts. Coders develop niche software tools that attract subscription-based revenue with minimal overhead. AI-enabled solopreneurs deploy automated workflows that accelerate product development, marketing, and customer management. Digital artisans monetise cultural content globally through creator platforms. Each of these examples showcases entrepreneurship decoupled from conventional business structures. Value is generated through capability, reach, and digital fluency rather than fixed capital or scale-dependent operations.The environments in which these actors operate differ markedly across geographies. In digitally advanced economies, high-bandwidth connectivity, predictable regulation, digital identity systems, and seamless online payments enable frictionless scale. Experimentation is lower-risk, compliance is structured, and digital infrastructure is widely accessible. In contrast, emerging and infrastructurally constrained environments present uneven connectivity, inconsistent regulatory enforcement, limited digital governance, and complex payment ecosystems. Yet the same distributed digital natives in these contexts often access global markets precisely because barriers to entry have collapsed. Their operating models do not rely on traditional domestic support structures, allowing them to circumvent institutional gaps that limit other forms of enterprise activity.

Platforms and AI are reshaping the logic of production itself. Cloud computing has pushed the cost of entry close to zero. Algorithmic tools execute tasks that once required specialised teams. Digital marketplaces provide instant access to international demand. Distributed project teams form around reputational signals, portfolio visibility, and digital trust rather than formal hiring structures. These dynamics are forging a model of entrepreneurship that is iterative, decentralised, and fundamentally network-centric.

This raises critical questions for policymakers, development planners, and institutions responsible for designing innovation ecosystems. Legacy support mechanisms—credit-based financing systems, physical incubation centres, collateral-driven lending, formal classification structures—were built for industries that required physical assets, linear growth paths, and sequential scaling. If distributed digital natives continue to expand as a defining force within global production, these frameworks risk becoming increasingly misaligned with the realities of digital value creation.

The real strategic challenge lies in recognising that capability, not capital, is becoming the primary driver of new-generation entrepreneurship. Digital identity systems, interoperable payment infrastructures, accessible cloud services, data governance frameworks, cross-border digital trade protocols, and digital skill-building initiatives determine whether ecosystems can support these emerging actors. Countries that focus narrowly on traditional enterprise assistance risk overlooking where the next wave of innovation and economic dynamism is actually taking place.The distributed digital native represents a new model of enterprise formation—one that is lean, globally integrated, and technologically amplified. It signals a shift from firm-based development to network-based productivity, where the boundaries between creator, entrepreneur, and digital worker continue to blur. Understanding and responding to this shift is crucial for nations seeking to build resilient, future-oriented innovation systems.

AI Data Center Networking Market: Building the Backbone of the AI-Driven Digital Economy

Chris Peterson

According to the latest research by Research Intelo, the global AI data center networking market was valued at USD 7.8 billion in 2024 and is projected to expand sharply to USD 41.6 billion by 2033, registering a robust compound annual growth rate (CAGR) of 20.5 percent during the forecast period from 2025 to 2033. This rapid expansion reflects the growing centrality of artificial intelligence workloads in modern digital infrastructure and the corresponding transformation of data center networking architectures.

**First published in the Web Edition of Global SME News <www.globalsmenews.com>*

AI Workloads and the Transformation of Data Center Networks

The AI data center networking market is increasingly recognized as a critical backbone of the contemporary digital economy. As enterprises deploy advanced artificial intelligence models for predictive analytics, automation, generative applications, and real-time decision-making, conventional data center networking systems are proving inadequate. AI workloads—particularly those associated with deep learning, large language models, and advanced analytics—require extremely high bandwidth, ultra-low latency, and seamless scalability.

Next-generation networking solutions are therefore being adopted to enable efficient data flow between graphics processing units (GPUs), AI accelerators, storage systems, and cloud platforms. These high-performance networks are essential for optimizing training and inference processes, reducing bottlenecks, and ensuring that AI systems deliver consistent and reliable performance at scale.

Market Growth and Key Demand Drivers

Several structural drivers are accelerating growth in the AI data center networking market. Foremost among them is the rapid advancement of AI technologies, including generative AI and large-scale neural networks, which dramatically increase east–west traffic within data centers. AI training workloads involve the continuous movement of massive datasets across interconnected computing nodes, placing unprecedented stress on existing networking infrastructure.

The expansion of hyperscale data centers is another significant growth driver. Technology firms and cloud service providers are investing heavily in large-scale facilities designed specifically to support AI-driven workloads. At the same time, AI adoption is broadening across multiple sectors, including healthcare, financial services, automotive manufacturing, and retail, each of which requires reliable, high-speed networking environments to support data-intensive applications.

The growing prevalence of cloud computing and hybrid data center models further reinforces demand. Enterprises increasingly rely on cloud-based AI services while retaining certain workloads on-premises, necessitating advanced networking frameworks capable of handling distributed architectures without compromising security, latency, or reliability.

Structural and Operational Challenges

Despite strong growth prospects, the AI data center networking market faces several notable challenges. High capital expenditure remains a key constraint, particularly for investments in advanced switches, optical interconnects, and AI-optimized networking hardware. For many organizations, especially mid-sized enterprises, the upfront costs of upgrading networking infrastructure can be substantial.

Integration with legacy data center systems presents an additional challenge. Many organizations operate mixed environments where traditional architectures must coexist with modern, high-speed AI networks, increasing deployment complexity and transition timelines. Rising energy consumption and heat generation associated with dense AI workloads further elevate operational costs, intensifying the need for efficient thermal management and power optimization.

Ensuring ultra-low latency, seamless scalability, and robust cybersecurity across distributed and hybrid environments also remains a persistent technical hurdle, particularly as AI workloads become more mission-critical.

Technological Innovations Reshaping the Market

Technological innovation continues to play a central role in shaping the evolution of AI data center networking. High-speed Ethernet, InfiniBand, advanced optical interconnects, and software-defined networking (SDN) are increasingly deployed to address congestion, enhance throughput, and support parallel processing at scale.

In parallel, AI-driven network automation is gaining traction. Intelligent network management platforms leverage machine learning algorithms to optimize traffic routing, predict hardware or performance failures, and dynamically allocate resources. This shift toward autonomous networking significantly reduces operational complexity, improves uptime, and enhances overall efficiency in large and complex data center environments.

Competitive Landscape

The competitive landscape of the AI data center networking market is characterized by the presence of major global technology providers, including:
Arista Networks

- Cisco Systems
- Juniper Networks
- Huawei Technologies

- NVIDIA Corporation
- Intel Corporation
- Broadcom Inc.
- Extreme Networks
- Dell Technologies
- Hewlett Packard Enterprise (HPE)

These firms are actively investing in high-speed networking solutions, AI-optimized hardware, and integrated platforms designed to meet the evolving requirements of AI-intensive data centers.

Future Outlook

The long-term outlook for the AI data center networking market remains highly positive. As artificial intelligence applications become more pervasive, data-intensive, and embedded across economic sectors, demand for ultra-fast, scalable, and intelligent networking solutions will continue to rise. Emerging domains such as edge AI and, over the longer term, quantum computing are expected to further elevate the strategic importance of data center networks.

In this context, AI data center networking is no longer a supporting component but a foundational enabler of next-generation digital ecosystems. Its continued evolution will be critical to sustaining innovation, competitiveness, and performance in an increasingly AI-driven global economy.

*The rise of eco-living: Why the demand for sustainable homes is accelerating in Indian cities***

Ruchit Mehta*

Luxury housing in India is undergoing a fundamental shift. What was once synonymous with grand foyers, imported fixtures and expansive amenities is now being redefined by sustainability, wellness and long-term value creation. The new markers of luxury in urban India are clean air, natural light, energy-efficient designs and responsible material use. This is not simply a lifestyle trend—it reflects a structural transformation underway in the country's residential real estate market.

Industry estimates show that India's green building segment is expanding at an

**Mr. Ruchit Mehta is the Partner, Mehta Realty*

***First published in the Web Edition of Global SME News*

unprecedented pace. The market is projected to grow from USD 37.99 billion in FY2024 to USD 85.00 billion by FY2032, at a CAGR of 10.59 per cent. This surge is driven by heightened environmental awareness, post-pandemic prioritisation of health, and the growing preference for homes that minimise both ecological impact and operating costs. Features such as improved ventilation, daylight optimisation, energy-efficient systems and water-saving fixtures—earlier treated as optional add-ons—have become central decision-making factors for homebuyers.

A generational shift

Millennials, who will make up more than 60 per cent of the global workforce by 2030, are now the dominant homebuying cohort in Indian cities. A 2023 survey found that nearly 75 per cent of millennials are willing to pay a premium for homes with sustainable value-adds. Knight Frank's research further indicates that HNIs, UHNIs and NRIs increasingly prefer green-certified properties.

While environmental consciousness plays a role, economic rationality is equally influential. Data from the Indian Green Building Council (IGBC) shows that certified green homes can deliver 30–50 per cent energy savings and up to 50 per cent water savings. For younger buyers in particular, the long-term reduction in household expenditure has become a compelling determinant of purchase decisions.

Greener, smarter

Advances in technology and supportive policy interventions have narrowed the gap between higher upfront costs and eventual payback. According to the CII Green Building Congress, the payback period for green investments has shortened to just three to five years.

The financial advantages extend well beyond utility savings. A JLL study reports that green-certified residential and commercial buildings in major metropolitan areas command 11 per cent higher rents and 21 per cent higher sales premiums. These assets also tend to appreciate faster, with green-certified properties attracting up to 15 per cent more investor interest and earning around 10 per cent higher rentals. Lower vacancy rates, stronger tenant retention, and resilience against market volatility make such properties particularly attractive in an uncertain global environment.

Regulatory push

India's policy ecosystem is strongly aligned with the country's green building ambitions. The Energy Conservation Building Code (ECBC), enforced by the Bureau of Energy Efficiency, sets mandatory efficiency standards that have already reduced energy consumption by up to 40 per cent in compliant buildings.

Several states—including Haryana, Rajasthan and Tamil Nadu—offer powerful incentives such as additional Floor Area Ratio (FAR), tax rebates and fast-track environmental clearances for projects certified by IGBC or GRIHA. The emergence of sustainable Real Estate Investment Trusts (REITs), with annual investments expected to cross 8,000 crore by 2025, reflects the growing institutional appetite for green assets.

The Real Estate Regulatory Authority (RERA) has also placed greater emphasis on sustainability, requiring developers to disclose green features and environmentally sound design elements in their project specifications. Complementary national programs such as the Smart Cities Mission, led by the Ministry of Housing and Urban Affairs, are embedding green building norms directly into urban development frameworks. These efforts collectively align India's real estate sector with the country's Net Zero 2070 commitment.

The new mainstream

Sustainable homes are no longer niche offerings; they are steadily becoming the preferred choice for urban buyers. Whether driven by immediate wellness considerations, mid-term savings or long-term asset appreciation, eco-friendly housing options now define the trajectory of India's residential real estate market.

Prospective buyers are advised to evaluate project certifications (such as IGBC or GRIHA), review sustainability features in detail, and request quantifiable estimates of anticipated savings on energy and water use. Such due diligence ensures that the benefits of green living fully translate into everyday experience and long-term financial value.

Eco-living is not simply a trend—it is the new foundation of urban housing in India, reflecting a future where luxury and sustainability are inseparable.

Why the Right Office Space Is a Competitive Advantage for SMEs

Hiren Chheda, Founder & Managing Director of Ekatva Group and Chairman, Commercial Development, MCHI Thane, underscores that selecting the right office space can shape an SME's growth as decisively as product innovation or market strategy. He notes that factors such as location, cost structure, and the surrounding business ecosystem influence credibility, talent attraction, and long-term value creation. Emerging hubs with strong infrastructure and room for expansion—such as Thane and other suburban business districts—demonstrate how strategic real estate decisions can turn office premises from a fixed expense into a lasting competitive advantage.

For a budding or established SME, an office space offers more than just an address to bookend the business – it is a cornerstone, lending credibility and the opportunity to foster an inspiring work environment. However, choosing the right office space becomes paramount especially in the case of SMEs, who must budget carefully to prevent overruns – while typical rental expenses range from 5-15 per cent of a company's overall operating budget, factors such as the industry, business model and the company stage make this decision very subjective. The following parameters will enable SMEs to determine how to select an office

*First published in the Web Edition of Global SME News**

space that doesn't eat into their finances, while contributing tangible business outcomes.

Emerging over established

In a city where real estate comes at a premium, the right location can not only yield cost savings but also make a significant impact on employees' mindset and productivity levels. While established business hubs such as Lower Parel and BKC can prove prohibitively expensive, upcoming locations such as Andheri East, Powai, Thane and Vikhroli can offer a far more competitive cost-to-benefits ratio. Thane is emerging as a hotspot for SMEs with 161,357 enterprises registered in the district as of June 2025, as per figures from the Udyam portal. An obvious and direct correlation that can be drawn is the difference in potential capital appreciation – as of Q1 2025, BKC's commercial office spaces are priced at an average of INR 45,000 per square foot while Thane's offices are more conservatively priced between INR 11,000 and INR13,000 per square foot. As the area continues to develop, the lower cost of acquisition will translate into a higher potential for capital appreciation.

Ease of expansion

With marquee commercial hotspots in Mumbai rapidly approaching saturation, companies are migrating to suburban business hubs such as Thane and Navi Mumbai, which are backed by excellent infrastructure, better planning and potential for further business expansion. These locations are largely considered as startup-friendly destinations, particularly for the IT, fintech, and logistics sectors. Growing businesses prioritise the availability of affordable office spaces, business parks and SEZs in these areas. Thane, for example, is projected to add 3.5 million sq. ft. of Grade A office space by the end of 2025, which will significantly increase its commercial footprint. For SMEs this becomes a great avenue to set up shop, as potential needs for larger office spaces can be easily fulfilled. Compare this to hubs like Andheri, BKC, Lower Parel where the struggle to increase office space is getting more challenging, due to limited new inventory additions and legacy businesses that have set up shop for decades.

Exceptional connectivity

For SMEs, there are two problems with hiring talent – the organization's perceived brand value and office location where employees will come to work. While the former is in itself a journey to build a better employer brand, the latter is much more in control for SMEs to optimize. Take Wagle Estate, Thane city's upcoming commercial district for example. With great connectivity from both Thane and Mulund railway stations, and enhance road connectivity via LBS Road and Eastern Express Highway, organizations have had no need to think twice when setting up office operations here. Additionally, with the upcoming Thane ring metro and Metro Line 4 of the MMRCL, connectivity for residents within the city and to other neighbouring suburbs will be enhanced. When organizations choose to set up their offices keeping future infrastructure upgrades in mind, they set the correct track to long term expansion and value appreciation for themselves. A quick employee demographic analysis of your organization will help you to better address employee's travel routes and thereby help identify the right office location for you.

A productive mindset

It is imperative for commercial spaces to be complemented by high quality residential properties, open spaces and robust social infrastructure, all of which contribute to a better quality of life for employees residing in the area and can improve their motivation and productivity levels. In Thane where we have delivered over a million sqft of commercial spaces, I see this sentence play out every day. Businesses need three things to flourish – residential pockets where potential customers live, social infrastructure where customers from further away can be pulled, and other businesses that increase the likelihood of potential customers to engage with some organizations in the larger network. In Wagle Estate alone, there are currently more than 2000 small, medium and large enterprises with offices, catering to all kinds of industries and sectors. For SMEs, having an ecosystem helps in many ways. Professionals needed to hire for consulting, audit and other services already operate around you. Potential B2B customers are within arm's length of you. Acquiring new customers by building partnerships and reaching for references becomes much easier. While in pockets like BKC, either you have to be too large or too niche to make a space for yourself. After all, what is better for your productivity? Seeing a large MNC do 20% more revenue in a year or seeing your neighbouring office owner increase their sales by 20%?

Acquiring a good office space should be an especially careful consideration for SMEs. While cost optimisation is key, understanding one's business's needs and potential for expansion, while taking into account practical considerations such as employee wellbeing can enable businesses to convert their offices into assets.

Why BRICS Nations Are the Real Advanced Economies

Perumal Koshy

For decades, global development discourse has relied on outdated binaries—"developed" and "developing"—shaped by the post-World War II institutional architecture and Cold War geopolitics. The transatlantic powers of North America and Western Europe have long assumed the role of global standard-bearers of development. However, a closer look at present-day realities reveals a different story. On key indicators of state capacity, human capital, technological innovation, public service delivery, and urban resilience, the BRICS nations—Brazil, Russia, India, China, South Africa—and their expanding circle of partners are increasingly setting the pace.

Human Capital and the STEM Dividend

In human capital and education, BRICS countries exhibit striking gains. Russia maintains a literacy rate above 99%, with universities producing world-class engineers and scientists. China now leads globally in the number of STEM graduates, having rapidly reshaped its education system to meet the needs of AI, robotics, quantum computing, and biotech sectors.

India presents an equally compelling case. With over two million engineering graduates annually and a vast reservoir of medical and scientific professionals, it is fast emerging as a global talent powerhouse. Institutions like the IITs and AIIMS symbolize meritocratic excellence, with increasing outreach across socio-economic divides.

In contrast, several Western education systems face headwinds. Student debt, stagnation in math and science performance, and shortages of critical skills have raised alarms. The United States, for example, has over 40 million adults with limited literacy, while Europe grapples with an ageing workforce and bureaucratic inertia in higher education.

Industrial Strength, Strategic Autonomy, and Innovation

Beyond talent, BRICS economies are leveraging this human capital to achieve strategic industrial autonomy. Russia's defense-industrial sector has demonstrated resilience despite sanctions, sustaining production efficiently. India's push for self-reliance through "Make in India" is bearing fruit, including breakthroughs in space technology and defense exports. China, meanwhile, has become a global leader in

These nations are no longer passive adopters of Western innovations. Rather, they are incubating their own technology ecosystems. India's Unified Payments Interface (UPI), China's AI deployments in healthcare and transport, and Russia's homegrown software solutions highlight the emergence of innovation models that are adaptive, context-specific, and strategically autonomous.

Healthcare Delivery: An Indicator of State Capacity

Healthcare, a litmus test of effective governance, tells a similar story. Western systems—often lauded for their sophistication—are increasingly beset by rising costs, service delivery challenges, and declining accessibility. Millions in the United States remain un

In comparison, BRICS countries have made notable strides. India's healthcare sector combines public-private partnerships to offer quality care at globally competitive costs. China's AI-driven diagnostics and community-level care delivery are improving access in rural provinces. Russia's universal healthcare legacy continues to guarantee basic services across vast geographies. These systems, often marginalized in Western assessments, demonstrate greater cost-efficiency and broader outreach.

Urban Housing, Inequality, and the New Metropolis

Urban housing and inequality are further areas where BRICS nations challenge prevailing narratives. While homelessness and housing crises are becoming endemic in Western cities, many BRICS urban centers—despite structural challenges—have retained more inclusive housing access.

For instance, Russia's state housing programs continue to serve millions. In India, informal settlements, while lacking in amenities, nonetheless offer social cohesion, shelter, and proximity to employment—unlike the stark urban exclusion visible in encampments across Western metropolises. China's large-scale housing initiatives have transformed peri-urban zones into integrated urban habitats.

Though urban inequality persists, the architecture of social protection and shelter security is arguably more inclusive and accessible in many BRICS cities than in their Western counterparts.

Entrepreneurial Dynamism and Innovation at the Periphery

One of the most under-appreciated transformations is in entrepreneurial energy. India's startup ecosystem—supported by Aadhaar, UPI, and the Open Network for Digital Commerce (ONDC)—is fostering an innovation culture with local relevance. China's tech hubs in Shenzhen and Hangzhou are shaping global digital trends. Even under sanctions, Russia is fostering dual-use technology ventures and indigenous digital platforms.

Entrepreneurship in BRICS nations isn't mimicking Silicon Valley—it is evolving through frugal innovation, agile experimentation, and contextual problem-solving. These economies are producing scalable, resilient business models tailored to domestic challenges, often with global implications.

Emerging Global Centres of Gravity

BRICS countries are also becoming epicenters of global discourse. Their cities host leading business forums, summits, expos, and cultural festivals. From AI summits in Shanghai to G20 leadership in Delhi, these nations are increasingly anchoring global conversations.

Today, cities like Dubai, Delhi, Cape Town, São Paulo, and Shanghai attract greater—business and event footfall than many long-established "global cities" in the West. The geography of influence is shifting.

Development Reimagined

The West's claim to developmental supremacy was historically built on financial dominance, colonial extraction, and global institutional control. Post-war prosperity in Europe and North America, often mistaken for intrinsic superiority, was enabled by systemic imbalances in labor, capital, and trade.

That paradigm is now unraveling. BRICS nations are not simply "catching up." They are restructuring the fundamentals of development. The first world is no longer a geographic construct rooted in the West. It is a function of energy, creativity, state capacity, and societal resilience. In these domains, BRICS nations are not just participating—they are leading.

Psychology of Control

Perumal Koshy

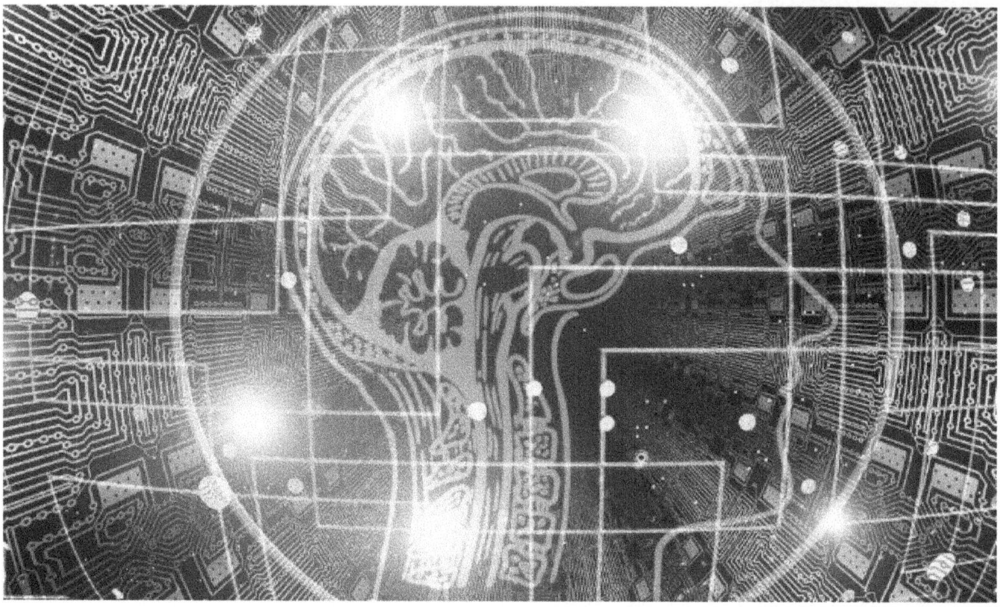

In times of crisis or transition, the temptation to cling to certainty becomes dangerously appealing. But when certainty turns into absolutism—the belief that "whatever I think, believe, or say is correct, and only my version is valid"—we cross into the realm of authoritarian psychology. This mindset, at its extreme, has historically laid the foundation for Fascism and Nazism. It dehumanizes others, rejects dialogue, and glorifies control.

What we often overlook is that this tendency doesn't begin in political parties or state structures. It begins with a psychological posture—a refusal to accept complexity, contradiction, or dissent. It begins when leaders or institutions refuse

*First published in the Web Edition of Global SME News**

to be questioned, when systems are designed to punish disagreement, and when criticism is treated as betrayal.

In the 1930s, this was the fertile ground that nurtured fascist ideologies. In our own times, it quietly creeps into corporate boardrooms, media narratives, social media algorithms, and enterprise culture.

Absolutism in Business Leadership

Enterprises today operate in dynamic, complex, and often uncertain environments. While decisiveness is a key entrepreneurial trait, it must not morph into ideological rigidity. Many small enterprises, family-owned businesses, and even startups suffer when founders or decision-makers adopt a belief in their infallibility—resisting input, shutting down team feedback, or refusing to adapt.

Authoritarian business environments often:

Penalize independent thinking;
Reward blind conformity;
Mislabel questions as disloyalty;
Foster burnout through micromanagement.

This mirrors, in form if not in scale, the same exclusionary logic that totalitarian ideologies imposed on society at large: there is only one right way, and it is mine.

The Economic Cost of Intolerance

Whether in politics or enterprise, absolutist thinking is not just ethically troubling—it is economically unsustainable. Diverse teams, inclusive leadership, and open systems of knowledge-sharing are now recognized as key drivers of innovation. In contrast, rigid hierarchies and top-down control systems limit adaptability and resilience.

The authoritarian mindset is not compatible with a 21st-century economy that depends on collaboration, networks, and co-creation. And yet, many sectors—especially where digital transitions, generational shifts, or political interference are at play—show signs of a growing intolerance toward difference, criticism, or alternative models.

Reclaiming Humility and Dialogue

Whether in a political party, a public institution, or a small enterprise, humility is the first line of defense against fascism. It is the recognition that no one has a monopoly on truth, that progress comes through dialogue, and that leadership includes the ability to listen—and to admit error.

In the business world, this humility shows up in:

- Participatory management approaches;
- Learning organizations that embrace feedback;
- Policies that center inclusion over uniformity.

A pluralistic enterprise culture is not only morally necessary—it is vital for long-term survival.

Fascism begins in the mind long before it shows up in public life. When we declare others wrong by default, dismiss opposing views as threats, or shut down spaces of dialogue, we begin to mirror the same absolutist tendencies that fueled the worst ideologies of the 20th century.

Today, as we navigate volatility across economies, societies, and belief systems, we must ask: Are we building cultures of fear and conformity—or ecosystems of trust, dialogue, and shared futures?

The choice is not merely political. It is deeply personal, professional, and moral.

Global Automotive Coatings Market Poised to Reach USD 29.1 Billion by 2032

The worldwide automotive coatings industry is projected to grow from USD 18.4 billion in 2024 to USD 29.1 billion by 2032, according to a new market study by Research Intelo. The report forecasts a 5.2 percent compound annual growth rate (CAGR) between 2025 and 2033, citing surging vehicle production, stringent environmental regulations, and rapid advances in coating technology as the key forces behind this expansion.

Demand Drivers
The ongoing boom in automobile manufacturing—especially across Asia-Pacific economies such as China and India—continues to lift demand for high-perfor-

*First published in the Web Edition of Global SME News**

mance coatings. Rising consumer preference for customized finishes, superior gloss, and corrosion resistance is further reshaping the competitive landscape.

Environmental compliance is another major catalyst. In response to stricter global rules on volatile organic compound (VOC) emissions, manufacturers are shifting from solvent-based products to waterborne and powder coatings, which meet sustainability targets while maintaining performance standards.

Technology and Product Mix

Automotive coatings cover four principal product types—electrocoat primers, basecoats, clearcoats, and primers—and employ technologies such as waterborne, solvent-borne, powder, and UV-cured systems. Innovations including nanotechnology, self-healing paints, and smart coatings capable of altering color or repairing micro-scratches are moving from the lab to the production line.

Regional Highlights

Asia-Pacific leads the market, supported by high vehicle output and rapid adoption of eco-friendly formulations.
North America shows steady growth, driven by advanced coatings for electric vehicles (EVs).
Europe enforces strict environmental regulations, accelerating demand for low-VOC and powder-coat solutions.
Latin America and the Middle East are experiencing gradual gains as urbanization and vehicle ownership rise.

Competitive Landscape

Major players such as PPG Industries, Axalta Coating Systems, BASF SE, Akzo Nobel N.V., Sherwin-Williams, Nippon Paint, Kansai Paint, Jotun, and KCC Corporation dominate the market, investing heavily in research, acquisitions, and new product development to maintain an edge.

Outlook

Despite headwinds from raw-material cost fluctuations and the capital requirements of transitioning to waterborne and powder technologies, Research Intelo projects strong long-term growth. Opportunities lie in EV-specific coatings, bio-based formulations, and energy-efficient curing processes, making automotive coatings a critical enabler of future mobility solutions.

As India's real estate sector enters 2026, growth is becoming more selective, infrastructure-anchored, and trust-driven. The next phase is defined less by scale and speculation, and more by integrated communities, redevelopment, and alignment with long-term urban systems. Public infrastructure investments, evolving buyer expectations, and stronger governance norms are reshaping where and how value is created. Developers who prioritise delivery discipline, connectivity, and community-centric design are emerging as leaders in a maturing market—signalling a decisive shift from volume-led expansion to strategic urban value creation.

Infrastructure-Led Growth, Integrated Communities, and the Trust Imperative

As India's real estate sector steps into 2026, the contours of growth are becoming clearer—and more disciplined. After a strong recovery phase marked by record registrations and renewed buyer confidence, the sector is now transitioning from expansion-driven momentum to a phase defined by infrastructure alignment, redevelopment, and long-term urban value creation. Developers across the Mumbai Metropolitan Region (MMR) point to a convergence of public infrastructure investment, evolving consumer expectations, and tighter governance standards as the forces shaping the next cycle. The emphasis is shifting decisively toward certainty, integrated living, and projects that are embedded within the broader urban system rather than isolated developments.

Voices from the Sector

Reflecting on this transition, Bhavesh Shah, Joint Managing Director of Today Group, observes that the sector is moving beyond scale alone.
"As we head into 2026, Indian real estate is moving from simple expansion to purpose-driven evolution. The next era will be shaped by integrated ecosystems, smarter last-mile connectivity, and a renewed focus on trust-led and sustainable development. Homebuyers today seek more than just homes — they want cer-

*First published in the Web Edition of Global SME News**

tainty, meaningful community, and a lifestyle that grows in long-term value."

A similar infrastructure-led outlook emerges from peripheral and emerging corridors. Jash Panchamia, Promoter, Suraksha Smart City, highlights how extended suburban regions are entering the spotlight.

"Mumbai's extended suburban areas led by Vasai's emergence as the 'Fourth Mumbai' will steer 2026 real estate trends. Mega townships with proximity to railway lines and the metro, use of precast technology, and forest-themed greens will define affordable, amenity-rich living."

Infrastructure, however, is not only about new regions but also about reshaping existing urban choices. Mayur R. Shah, Vice-Chairman, Marathon Nextgen Realty Ltd., underlines how transport projects are redrawing the residential map.
"Transformational infrastructure such as the Mumbai Trans Harbour Link, Metro Line 4, and new tunnel roads will dramatically cut commute times. These projects will change how people choose where to live and which micro-markets emerge next."

From a broader citywide perspective, Vivek Mohanani, CEO & MD, Ekta World, points to a three-fold convergence shaping 2026.
"Infrastructure, policy, and evolving consumer aspirations are coming together. Metro corridors, the coastal road extension, and the new airport at Navi Mumbai will unlock value, while redevelopment policies will ensure safer, modern homes for citizens."

Beyond infrastructure and redevelopment, technology and sustainability are becoming structural, not optional. Vishal Ratanghayra, Founder & CEO, Platinum Corp, notes:

"2026 will see deeper integration of AI-driven PropTech, a stronger push toward ESG-led sustainability, and the rise of asset classes such as senior living, co-living, and data centres. The sector is moving toward future-ready communities rather than standalone projects."

Cluster development within the city is another defining theme. Ruchit Mehta, Partner, Mehta Realty, explains:

"Western suburbs such as Malad, Goregaon, and Kandivali will witness growth driven by cluster developments that integrate homes, offices, and retail. These communities reduce commute times and enhance everyday living."

At the same time, buyer expectations are becoming more values-driven. Chintan Sheth, Chairman & Managing Director, Sheth Realty, reflects:

"Buyers today seek more than homes — they seek experiences rooted in wellbeing, transparency, and trust. The future belongs to those who build with intention and resilience."

Integrity and delivery discipline also remain central to the narrative. Aditya N. Shah, Director, Mayfair Housing, highlights:
"Timely occupation certificates, redevelopment, and mixed-use launches across MMR will underscore an integrity-driven ethos that supports sustainable urban transformation."

Finally, township-scale development and community-oriented formats are expected to gain further momentum. Anuj Goradia, Director, Dosti Realty, notes:
"Senior living, integrated townships, and community-focused developments supported by strong connectivity and social infrastructure will define MMR's next growth cycle."

What These Signals Indicate for 2026

Taken together, these perspectives reveal a sector entering a phase of consolidation and maturity. Infrastructure is no longer a background enabler but the primary demand trigger. Integrated townships and mixed-use clusters are emerging as practical responses to congestion, affordability pressures, and changing work-life patterns. Trust—expressed through timely delivery, regulatory compliance, and transparent governance—is becoming a decisive market differentiator. At the same time, technology adoption and ESG alignment are reshaping how projects are designed, built, and positioned.

The outlook for 2026 suggests that real estate growth will be measured less by volume and more by relevance to the urban system. Developers who align projects with infrastructure timelines, prioritise redevelopment and community living, and demonstrate delivery credibility are likely to lead the next cycle. For homebuyers and investors, the focus is shifting toward long-term liveability, resilience, and certainty. As Indian cities evolve, real estate is moving beyond asset creation toward the shaping of durable urban ecosystems—marking 2026 as a year of strategic maturity rather than speculative expansion.

Stability, Infrastructure Momentum, and the Emergence of a Market-Driven Cycle

Svetlana M

The Union Budget 2026–27 arrives at a moment when India's real estate sector is transitioning from a phase of post-pandemic recovery into one defined by consolidation, execution discipline, and infrastructure alignment. Unlike earlier budget cycles where industry expectations centred on tax incentives, affordability measures, or sector-specific stimulus, this year's policy approach signals continuity. The government has chosen to reinforce macroeconomic stability and long-term infrastructure investment rather than introduce direct interventions for housing demand or developer balance sheets.

Industry responses reflect a broad consensus that the budget neither significantly advances nor constrains the sector. Instead, it establishes a framework in which growth is expected to be shaped primarily by market fundamentals—buyer confidence, capital flows, infrastructure execution, and interest-rate trajectories. The absence of new incentives has therefore become the central analytical theme: real estate is being positioned as a sector capable of sustaining momentum without fiscal support, but one that must increasingly rely on structural drivers rather than policy-led expansion.

A Budget of Continuity Rather Than Intervention

From the standpoint of residential real estate, several industry voices interpret Budget 2026 as neutral in immediate impact. Ruchit Mehta, Partner, Mehta

*First published in the Web Edition of Global SME News**

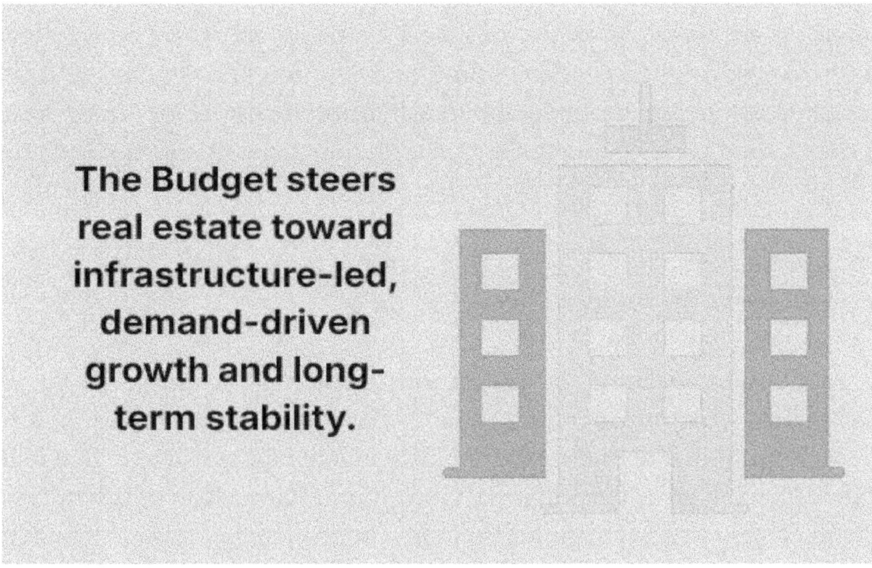

Realty, notes that homebuyers had anticipated meaningful relief, but the continuation of existing tax and policy norms suggests that the government views the sector as sufficiently stable. With residential sales already strong and personal finance conditions largely unchanged, any near-term momentum, in this view, will depend more on market sentiment and equity performance than on policy stimulus.

This reading is reinforced by Aditya N. Shah, Joint Managing Director, Mayfair Housing, who similarly observes that there is nothing materially new for either real estate developers or homebuyers in the budget. However, he emphasises that the sector enters this phase from a position of strength. If consumer sentiment and capital markets remain supportive, housing demand may continue along its existing trajectory, making this a budget that relies on confidence rather than fiscal intervention to sustain growth.

A more critical assessment comes from Parthh K. Mehta, CMD, Paradigm Realty, who describes the absence of fresh incentives or policy recalibration as a missed opportunity. According to this perspective, the government appears to be betting on organic demand and market momentum rather than actively addressing affordability concerns or expanding homebuyer incentives. This view is echoed by Vishal Ratanghayra, Founder & CEO, Platinum Corp., who notes that while broader reforms and economic stability support confidence, industry expectations around higher income-loan interest deduction caps and industry recognition remain unaddressed.

Taken together, these responses indicate a sector adjusting to a new policy reality. Rather than relying on periodic stimulus measures, developers are increasingly expected to operate within stable but non-interventionist policy frameworks. The implication is clear: execution capability, financial discipline, and alignment with long-term urban trends will matter more than policy-driven demand creation.

Infrastructure as the Central Growth Engine

If there is one area where industry responses converge strongly, it is the recognition that infrastructure spending remains the most significant indirect driver of real estate growth. The increase in public capital expenditure to 12.2 lakh crore is widely interpreted as reinforcing the structural foundation of urban expansion. Bhavesh Shah, Joint Managing Director, Today Group, views the budget's emphasis on infrastructure as a positive signal that strengthens long-term demand fundamentals. Connectivity improvements and urban development continue to shape housing demand patterns, particularly in infrastructure-led growth corridors such as Navi Mumbai and Panvel. In this context, the absence of disruptive policy changes provides continuity and clarity, enabling developers to plan with greater certainty.

Similarly, Chintan Sheth, Chairman and Managing Director, Sheth Realty, highlights the strengthening of India's urban transformation backbone through sustained investment in infrastructure and connectivity.

The expansion of high-speed rail and urban infrastructure is expected to enhance the attractiveness of emerging micro-markets while supporting premium and lifestyle-oriented developments. The additional push toward domestic manufacturing of advanced infrastructure equipment—from elevators to safety systems—is also seen as a step toward improving construction quality, reliability, and cost efficiency, aligning Indian real estate with global benchmarks.

This infrastructure-led narrative is reinforced by Anuj Goradia, Director, Dosti Realty, who emphasises that improved connectivity and increased public capex directly enhance urban liveability and support large-scale township developments across Tier I, II, and III cities. Infrastructure expansion not only drives residential demand but also reshapes the geography of development by unlocking new corridors for growth.

Financing, Risk Mitigation, and Execution Certainty

One of the more structurally significant announcements in the budget—the proposed Infrastructure Risk Guarantee Fund—has drawn particular attention from industry stakeholders concerned with project financing and execution risks. For a sector where delays and funding constraints have historically affected delivery timelines, improved lender confidence carries substantial implications.

Prashant Khandelwal, Joint Secretary of CREDAI MCHI and CEO of Agami Realty, notes that the fund could accelerate infrastructure completion and improve access to capital, thereby supporting real estate growth through enhanced connectivity. He also points to the proposed recycling of Central Public Sector Enterprise (CPSE) real estate assets through REIT structures as a positive move that could unlock underutilised land resources in land-constrained cities such as Mumbai.

Samyag M. Shah, Director, Marathon Nextgen Realty Ltd, similarly underscores that improved project financing mechanisms can bring greater certainty to execution and delivery outcomes. Funds have long been a key challenge for the sector, and risk-sharing mechanisms that improve credit access may contribute to smoother project completion cycles, benefiting both developers and homebuyers.

The broader implication of these measures is a gradual institutionalisation of real estate financing, where risk mitigation tools and capital recycling mechanisms play a larger role in sustaining sectoral growth than direct fiscal incentives.

Redevelopment, Urban Density, and Policy Stability

For cities such as Mumbai, where redevelopment remains central to future housing supply, industry responses emphasise the importance of policy continuity rather than short-term announcements. Sanjay Daga, CEO and Managing Director, Anex Advisory, frames redevelopment as a long-cycle process where confidence emerges from consistent policy execution, infrastructure investment, and administrative clarity. In dense urban environments, where projects extend across multiple years, stable regulatory frameworks become a decisive factor influencing investment decisions.

The monetisation of public land assets through REIT structures also intersects with this redevelopment narrative. By enabling more efficient use of existing land resources, the policy has the potential to improve land availability while encouraging mixed-use and integrated developments in urban centres facing land scarcity.

Digital Infrastructure and the Expanding Definition of Real Estate

An emerging dimension highlighted in industry responses is the growing intersection between real estate and digital infrastructure. Hardik Pandit, Director, APICES Studio Pvt. Ltd., draws attention to the long-term tax holiday for foreign cloud firms operating through Indian data centres, describing it as a strategic shift in how urban environments are conceived. As data centres become integral to economic infrastructure, architectural and planning priorities increasingly include energy efficiency, cooling systems, power reliability, and connectivity resilience.

This evolution reflects a broader transformation in the built environment, where real estate development extends beyond residential and commercial spaces to include digital infrastructure supporting the data economy. Cities such as Mumbai may increasingly position themselves as digital infrastructure hubs, influencing both land use patterns and construction standards.

Affordable Housing and the Question of Inclusion

Despite broad acceptance of the infrastructure-focused approach, industry feedback consistently returns to the question of affordability. Several stakeholders emphasise that affordable housing continues to hold multiplier effects for employment, consumption, and social stability.

Jash Panchamia, Promoter, Suraksha Smart City, notes that infrastructure expansion combined with improved financing mechanisms can enhance the viability of affordable housing projects, particularly in Tier II and Tier III cities. Faster infrastructure development and improved access to financing may make projects more accessible for end users while supporting sustainable urban growth.

Similarly, Suhan Shetty, Industrialist and Founder of Rubics Group, highlights that measures such as the Infrastructure Risk Guarantee Fund and the recycling of CPSE land assets could stimulate holistic growth by improving project viability and reducing input costs through stronger domestic manufacturing of construction equipment. These factors, while indirect, contribute to making homeownership more attainable over time.

Yet the recurring industry observation remains that direct affordability incentives were largely absent. This underscores a policy assumption that structural improvements in infrastructure and financing will gradually translate into affordability gains, rather than relying on immediate fiscal measures.

A Sector Moving Toward Market Discipline

Viewed collectively, the responses to Budget 2026 reveal a sector entering a new phase of maturity. The government's policy stance suggests confidence in real estate's existing momentum while signalling that future growth must increasingly emerge from infrastructure alignment, capital efficiency, and execution quality rather than periodic policy stimulus.

The budget therefore reinforces an ongoing transition. Indian real estate is moving from a policy-sensitive growth model toward one shaped by market discipline and long-term urban transformation. Developers capable of aligning projects with infrastructure corridors, managing capital prudently, and delivering quality with consistency are likely to benefit most from this environment.

Budget 2026 may ultimately be remembered not for headline announcements but for consolidating this shift. By prioritising stability, infrastructure investment, and institutional mechanisms over short-term incentives, it places responsibility for the sector's next phase of expansion squarely within the dynamics of market confidence and execution capability.

Cloud Skill Labs for Enterprises Market is Projected to Reach $9.8 billion by 2033.

Svetlana M

The Global Cloud Skill Labs for Enterprises Market, valued at USD 2.3 billion in 2024, is projected to reach USD 9.8 billion by 2033 at a CAGR of 17.3%, driven by accelerating digital transformation and rising demand for hands-on cloud training. As enterprises shift to hybrid and multi-cloud environments, Cloud Skill Labs enable immersive, real-world learning—bridging the gap between theory and practice. Powered by AI-driven adaptive learning, LMS integration, and gamified simulations, these platforms are transforming enterprise upskilling, certification readiness, and remote workforce enablement across industries like finance, healthcare, and manufacturing.

According to Research Intelo, the Global Cloud Skill Labs for Enterprises Market was valued at USD 2.3 billion in 2024 and is projected to reach USD 9.8 billion by 2033, expanding at a robust CAGR of 17.3% during 2024–2033. This rapid growth underscores a clear industry reality: as digital transformation accelerates, enterprises are investing heavily in scalable, hands-on cloud training ecosystems to future-proof their workforce.

As organizations increasingly migrate critical workloads to the cloud, the demand for continuous workforce upskilling and real-world, scenario-based learning environments has surged. The combination of advancing cloud technologies and a persistent shortage of skilled professionals has turned Cloud Skill Labs into a strategic enterprise imperative—vital for maintaining competitiveness, innovation, and compliance in an evolving digital economy.
The Rise of Cloud Skill Labs

*First published in the Web Edition of Global SME News**

In today's hybrid and multi-cloud world, enterprises face an urgent need to reskill and upskill employees in next-generation cloud technologies. Cloud Skill Labs have emerged as a practical solution, providing immersive, hands-on training environments where employees can safely experiment, deploy applications, and troubleshoot real-world challenges—without risking live production systems.

By bridging the gap between theoretical learning and practical application, these labs create a dynamic, experiential model of learning—one that aligns closely with enterprise needs for agility, scalability, and performance.

Key Market Drivers

1. Accelerating Cloud Adoption Across Industries

Sectors such as banking, manufacturing, healthcare, and retail are moving mission-critical workloads to the cloud. This migration demands a skilled workforce capable of managing, optimizing, and securing new digital infrastructures. Cloud Skill Labs offer an efficient, scalable, and cost-effective solution for organizations to build this capability internally—eliminating reliance on traditional, classroom-based training models.

2. Shift Toward Continuous Learning and Certification

Cloud certifications from AWS, Microsoft, and Google have become key benchmarks of professional competence. Cloud Skill Labs now embed curated exercises mapped to official certification syllabi, enabling faster skill validation and improved learning outcomes.

3. Demand for Real-World, Simulation-Based Learning

Traditional e-learning models often fail to deliver the interactivity needed to master complex architectures. Cloud Skill Labs address this gap by recreating realistic enterprise scenarios—such as deploying Kubernetes clusters, implementing CI/CD pipelines, or managing serverless environments—offering a truly experiential journey.

4. Remote and Hybrid Work Enablement

The post-pandemic workforce demands flexible, location-independent learning.

Cloud-based labs are inherently accessible from anywhere, allowing distributed teams to participate in standardized training. This flexibility has been a major driver of enterprise adoption.

Market Challenges

Despite their promise, Cloud Skill Labs face several challenges. Establishing secure, scalable lab environments requires ongoing investment in infrastructure and cloud credits. Data security and compliance remain pressing concerns—especially in highly regulated industries such as finance and healthcare. Additionally, balancing automation with human mentorship is a continuing challenge; while self-paced labs enhance flexibility, guided feedback is often crucial for effective learning.

Technology Trends Shaping the Market

AI-Powered Adaptive Learning

Artificial intelligence is revolutionizing cloud training delivery. Modern Cloud Skill Labs leverage AI to monitor learner performance, identify skill gaps, and recommend personalized learning paths—making training adaptive, efficient, and results-driven.

Integration with Enterprise Learning Management Systems (LMS)

Integration with enterprise LMS platforms ensures a unified experience—enabling centralized progress tracking, compliance reporting, and alignment with broader organizational learning initiatives.

Gamification and Collaborative Learning

To enhance engagement, leading providers incorporate gamified elements such as badges, leaderboards, and team-based challenges. Collaborative labs also mimic real-world DevOps teamwork, improving both technical and soft skills.

Edge and Multi-Cloud Learning Environments

As hybrid and multi-cloud adoption grows, Cloud Skill Labs are evolving to simulate cross-cloud operations and edge computing scenarios. This helps learners understand orchestration, interoperability, and distributed cloud management—

key skills in modern enterprise IT.

Future Outlook

The future of the Cloud Skill Labs for Enterprises Market looks exceptionally promising. With sustained double-digit growth projected through 2033, the market will continue to expand in tandem with innovations in generative AI, edge computing, and automation.

Next-generation labs are expected to integrate real-time analytics, transforming skill development into a measurable component of enterprise intelligence. As organizations mature into cloud-native enterprises, the focus will shift toward rapid experimentation, security-by-design, and AI-assisted operations—all of which will be supported by evolving cloud lab infrastructures.

Ultimately, Cloud Skill Labs are not just training tools—they are strategic assets that enable continuous innovation, workforce resilience, and digital agility.

Competitive Landscape

Prominent companies driving innovation in the Cloud Skill Labs for Enterprises Market include: Amazon Web Services (AWS); Microsoft Azure; Google Cloud Platform (GCP); IBM Cloud; Oracle Cloud; Salesforce; Alibaba Cloud; SAP; Pluralsight; Coursera for Business; Udemy Business; Cloud Academy; A Cloud Guru.

These players are continuously enhancing their offerings through AI integration, certification alignment, and enterprise-level partnerships to meet the evolving needs of the digital workforce.

As enterprises race to close the cloud skills gap, Cloud Skill Labs are emerging as the cornerstone of next-generation workforce development. Combining scalability, interactivity, and real-world application, they empower organizations to navigate digital transformation confidently and competitively.

The decade ahead will define how effectively enterprises can turn cloud proficiency into innovation—and Cloud Skill Labs will be at the heart of that transformation.

www.ingramcontent.com/pod-product-compliance
Ingram Content Group UK Ltd.
Pitfield, Milton Keynes, MK11 3LW, UK
UKHW061539190726
13845UKWH00031B/1122